Contents

Appendix

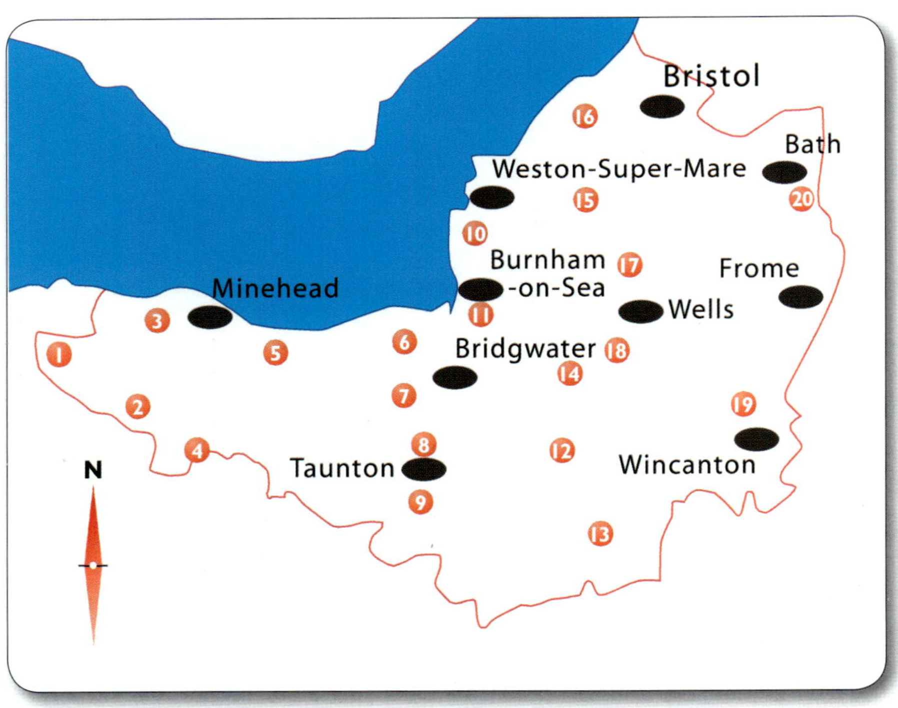

Area map showing location of the walks.

Somerset

A DOG WALKER'S GUIDE

Roger Evans

COUNTRYSIDE BOOKS

NEWBURY BERKSHIRE

INTRODUCTION

I know of no better way of meeting and making new friends than going out for a walk with my dog. I also enjoy a pint or two and appreciate those pubs where dogs are welcome. Somehow people who would never dream of starting a conversation in the middle of an open moorland or in a bar find no inhibitions when you have a dog. It's the dog that breaks the ice – 'Isn't he lovely!' or 'What's her name?' Whether it's in my home county or elsewhere, the dog is the one that makes friends – and I am grateful. I am convinced that dog walkers have more friends just because they are dog walkers.

Every year my wife and I enjoy at least two U.K. holidays where we take our dog with us. We head for the hills and the woodlands, so the Lake District, the New Forest, Dartmoor and such places attract us, locations where our dog can run free. We normally buy one or two walking books to help select routes but generally find them lacking those vital bits of information essential to dog walkers, such as: are the stiles they mention dog-friendly, with flaps to lift to allow dogs through, or are they those metal ones that threaten to break a dog's leg if he jumps it badly?

Our border collie, Buster, who is my constant walking companion, can jump almost any stile but, on occasions, I go out with a pack that consists of Buster, two springer spaniels, three border terriers and an Irish wolfhound! Now the wolfhound doesn't do stiles and even the dog-flaps aren't built for her enormous size. Suddenly walks that seemed a good idea with an agile border collie turn into a disappointment. Likewise, areas of woodland where pheasants have been released for shooting can spell disaster when running a springer spaniel. The world needs a series of 'Dog Walker's Guides'.

Somerset provides wonderful walking country with plenty of ancient woodland as well as forestry paths, where dogs can explore the scent trails left by squirrels and the deer, open moorland on Exmoor and the Quantocks, the Mendip and Blackdown Hills, even mile after mile of sandy beaches. It's a dog walker's paradise. It is essential, however, to use your own judgement as to when it is safe to let your dog off the lead. Please read the notes overleaf that are for your guidance.

In this volume I have carefully selected walks from across the county where stiles, sheep and cattle are at a minimum, if present at all. I also include details of where refreshments can be found, selecting only those places where I have found dogs to be welcome.

Enjoy your walks!

Roger Evans

ADVICE FOR DOG WALKERS

'The countryside is a great place to exercise dogs, but it is every owner's duty to make sure their dog is not a danger or nuisance to farm animals, wildlife or other people.' *(Taken from the Government's 'Code for the Public.' The full code is available on the Government's Countryside Access website: www.countrysideaccess.gov.uk)*

Please also note the following:

■ Large areas of Somerset, high moorland, low moorland and woodland, are home to ground nesting birds that need to be left undisturbed through the nesting season, which is March to July inclusive. Around September is the time when pheasants are released in their hundreds into woodland and open moorland for the shooting season. This is particularly the case on Exmoor and the Quantocks. Please observe any notices in such areas which typically will advise that dogs should be kept on a lead.

■ Sheep and lambs, generally speaking, will instinctively move away from dogs. Unfortunately some dogs find that fun and like to give chase. This can cause lambs to abort (January to March is lambing time) and livestock owners are entitled by law to shoot dogs worrying livestock. You may see notices that dogs worrying sheep will be shot.

■ Cattle are generally inquisitive and will move towards dogs, forming a semi-circle as they approach you. They are not generally harmful but a cow who considers her calf to be threatened may behave aggressively. In such cases, drop the dog lead and let the dog sort itself out. It is safer for both you and the dog. Because my border collie is obedience trained, I can put him in the down position before I enter a field containing cattle, even a bull. I then cross the field on my own and call him as I am leaving the field. He moves faster than any cattle and is generally out of the field before they notice.

■ There are plenty of wild ponies in Somerset, particularly on the Quantock Hills and Exmoor. I have never known them take any notice of people or their dogs – they simply move away if approached and are not, in my experience, any nuisance to dogs or their walkers.

■ The Quantock Hills and Exmoor are both plagued with ticks. Take note of the comments given below.

Ticks and Lyme Disease

Ticks will be found in plentiful numbers in Somerset especially on Exmoor and the Quantock Hills where sheep and deer roam freely. They feed off these animals until fully bloated and then drop off. They tend to cling to the edge of scrub plants, particularly bracken. Dogs running through bracken and undergrowth and, especially if they stop and lie down on open moorland, are liable to pick up ticks. Both dogs and humans are susceptible to them and you don't feel them bite. They can carry Lyme Disease, which should always be treated by a doctor. However, you can help to avoid tick bites by taking the following advice:

- Wear long trousers, tucked into socks, and long-sleeved shirts – even in hot weather.
- Light-coloured clothing makes the ticks easier to spot. They appear to be black or dark brown in colour.
- Always check yourself and your dog at the end of a walk. The ticks are easy to brush off as long as they haven't attached themselves.
- Insect repellents for dogs may help.
- If a tick has attached itself, it can generally be removed by getting the tips of your finger nails beneath the tick's body, as close to the skin as possible, and twisting them anti-clockwise. Twisting the tick clockwise is liable to snap the body away from the head, leaving the head embedded. Plastic 'Tick removers' may be safer for the less experienced and can be purchased at most Somerset vets.
- Most tourist information offices and tea rooms in the infected areas will carry free leaflets advising on the symptoms of Lyme Disease, which generally speaking are flu-like to begin but can have serious complications if not treated.

PUBLISHER'S NOTE

We hope that you obtain considerable enjoyment from this book; great care has been taken in its preparation. Although at the time of publication all routes followed public rights of way or permitted paths, diversion orders can be made and permissions withdrawn.

We cannot, of course, be held responsible for such diversion orders and any inaccuracies in the text which result from these or any other changes to the routes nor any damage which might result from walkers trespassing on private property. We are anxious though that all details covering the walks are kept up to date and would therefore welcome information from readers which would be relevant to future editions.

The simple sketch maps that accompany the walks in this book are based on notes made by the author whilst checking out the routes on the ground. They are designed to show you how to reach the start, to point out the main features of the overall circuit and they contain a progression of numbers that relate to the paragraphs of the text.

However, for the benefit of a proper map, we do recommend that you purchase the relevant Ordnance Survey sheet covering your walk. The Ordnance Survey maps are widely available, especially through booksellers and local newsagents.

The Doone Valley

Cloud Farm passed at point 4 of the walk.

This is a truly beautiful walk into the heart of some of Exmoor's most remote and inspiring landscapes. For 5 miles it explores the area where R. D. Blackmore based his novel *Lorna Doone*, where the boundaries are as vague between fact and fiction as they are between Devon and Somerset along this border of the counties. It is easy to see how this wild and romantic setting inspired such an enduring book.

The trail takes you along the valley that carries Badgworthy (pronounced Badgery) Water before, having discovered the true Doone Valley, heading back to reach the tea rooms at Cloud Farm, well worth a visit. From there the route heads uphill, crossing the high moor with its enclosed fields, before dropping down alongside a wood to reach Oare church, where Lorna Doone was shot by Carver Doone on the day of her wedding. Blackmore's grandfather was once the rector at Oare. As you walk there is a good chance of spotting red deer and the elusive dipper – in fact I have seen more dippers along this stretch of water than anywhere else in Somerset.

This is a great walk for dogs, where they can run free through deciduous woodland, dipping in and out of the stream along the way. It is perhaps best to keep your dogs on a lead for the first few yards whilst crossing the quiet metalled road at the start but they can then run free, at least until reaching the short stretch of fields on the homeward leg.

Terrain

Mostly riverside tracks, stony in places, through an enclosed valley and, later, enclosed moorland. Some minor ascents and descents but nothing too demanding.

Where to park

The village pay and display car park behind the shop in Malmsmead (GR 791477). **OS map:** Explorer OL9 Exmoor.

How to get there

From the A39 between Porlock and Lynmouth, take the road signposted to Oare, just on the Somerset side of the Devon/Somerset border. Follow this narrow road to the T-junction at Oare, near the church, and turn right to head to Malmsmead where the large car park with toilets will be found behind the village shop.

Nearest refreshments

Cloud Farm tea rooms, on the route, come well recommended and are open throughout the year. Overlooking the picturesque Badgworthy Water, they offer everything from cream teas to full meals, even breakfast. Their ample gardens provide plenty of space for dogs and there is also a small shop. Winter times are 11 am to 4 pm; summer 8.30 am to 5.30 pm (8 pm in the summer holidays). ☎ 01598 741278.

Dog factors

Distance: 5 miles.
Road walking: 600 yards of quiet lanes.
Livestock: Possibility of the odd sheep in the woodland stretch but generally they are not seen, being on the higher moorland. Popular with horse riders but the paths are wide, providing plenty of passing room.
Stiles: None.
Nearest vets: White Lodge Veterinary Clinic, Minehead

The Walk

1. On leaving the car park, head south along the road, which is signed as 'Public Footpath to **Doone Valley**'. Be sure to ignore the signposted short-cut whose purpose is to collect money from you for the privilege. You will be keeping the river known as **Badgworthy Water** on your left. Follow this road uphill until it bears to the right.

2. As the road bears right, leave it and continue straight ahead onto a waymarked public bridleway (**Badgworthy Valley**), still keeping the river deep down on your left-hand side. Continue for ½ mile.

Buster by the Blackmore memorial in the Doone Valley

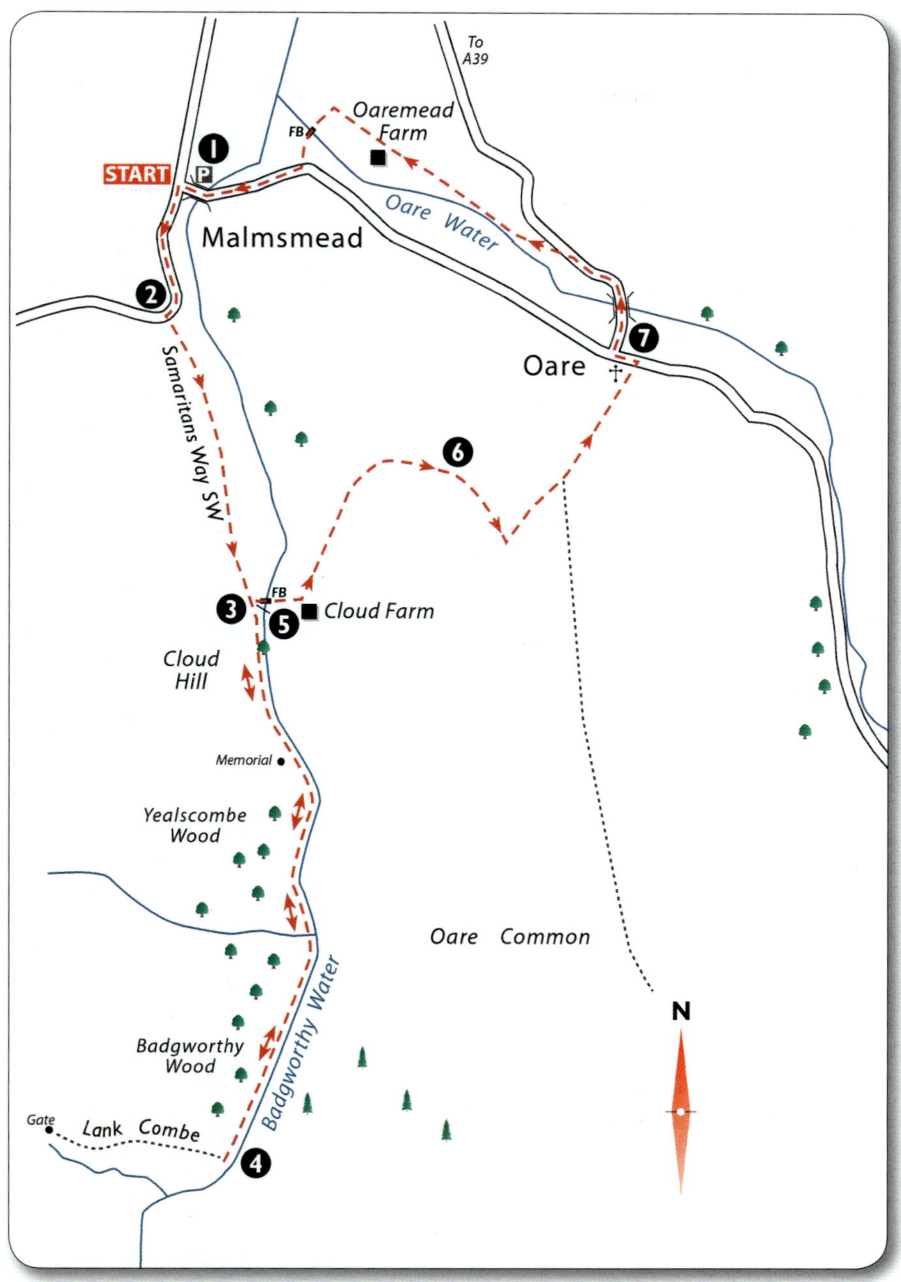
To A39
Oaremead Farm
FB
1
START
P
Malmsmead
Oare Water
2
Samaritans Way SW
Oare
7
6
FB
3
5
Cloud Farm
Cloud Hill
Memorial
Yealscombe Wood
Oare Common
Badgworthy Water
Badgworthy Wood
Gate
Lank Combe
4
N

3 After crossing a stream and passing through two gates, you come to a bridge which crosses the river – you will use this on your return leg but for now keep straight ahead through the steep-sided combe. In about 500 yards you will reach the memorial to R.D. Blackmore. Continue ahead through a gate where a fence crosses the river. Go past a signpost for '**Sir Hugh's Ride**', to where the path splits three ways. Whilst many believe the combe you have just walked along is the **Doone Valley**, it is the one to your right, **Lank Combe**, that can lay claim to the title.

4 Turn right onto a track which heads up **Lank Combe**, with the stream on your left-hand side, to reach a grassy area beyond which a gate crosses your path and the fence line is extended across the water. It is here that Jan Ridd entered the valley of the Doones. It may not seem very impressive in the summer months when the water level is low, but it becomes a torrent after substantial rainfall.

Having completed your 'Doone Pilgrimage', retrace your steps back down to **Badgworthy Water** and turn left along your former track to reach the bridge at point 3. Turn right to cross the footbridge, heading towards **Cloud Farm** and its tea rooms.

5 Make for the red phone box to the left of the farm and then bear left onto the footpath signposted to **Oare church**, passing through a barn, by the riding stables, with a gate at each end as you do so. Follow the track beyond the barn as it climbs uphill and go through a gate. Keep to the left-hand field boundary as the track bears right, passing the ruins of former sheep pens.

6 In the next field, follow the left-hand field boundary to a gate waymarked in yellow. Turn left through the gate onto a track along the woodland edge. Follow this as it turns left, signposted 'Footpath **Oare**', keeping to the edge of the trees. In about 100 yards, where the main track bears right, continue straight ahead and downhill through waymarked gates and follow this path down to the road at **Oare church**.

7 Turn left onto the road and then turn right, signposted to **Porlock**. In 120 yards you cross **Oare Water** and a few yards further on turn left through a five-bar wooden field gate onto a footpath signposted to **Malmsmead**. Continue along this path, passing to the right of **Oaremead Farm**, after which you bear left to cross an arched bridge over the river. Continue ahead to reach the road at **Parsonage Farm**. Turn right to reach the car park.

Tarr Steps

The River Barle.

At just two miles long, reasonably level throughout and passing through stunning scenery, short and sweet describes this walk well. The valley of the Barle is both charming and dramatic at all times of the year and the river runs beneath the ancient monument of Tarr Steps which can boast the finest clapper bridge in England, reaching across 180 ft of water in seventeen spans of flat stones. It was probably built more than 1,000 years BC, and the giant stones that form this ancient crossing place can weigh as much as five tons each.

This delightful route hugs the river bank as it passes through deciduous woodland. Grey wagtails (which are as much yellow as grey) can be seen running over the river boulders whilst the rarely seen dipper swims in between them. What makes an ideal walk for dogs? A place where they can run harmlessly off the lead, where they can follow a squirrel scent, swim in clear waters and where there is a toilet at the start and finish. Yes, this walk can even boast a DOG toilet at the car park, a fenced area set aside and signposted for that purpose. That's when you really know that dogs are welcome!

Terrain

Predominantly riverside gravel tracks with just a few gradual inclines. Firm underfoot and generally good even after wet weather.

Where to park

The pay and display car park up the hill from Tarr Steps (GR 872323). There are good clean toilet facilities here. **OS map:** Explorer OL9 Exmoor.

How to get there

Take the B3223, which runs between Simonsbath and Dulverton. About 5 miles north of Dulverton, turn off to head west, following the brown tourist signposts

Dog factors

Distance: 2 miles.
Road walking: 50 yards – very quiet.
Livestock: None, other than occasionally sheep along the first 100 yards.
Stiles: None.
Nearest vets: Dulverton Veterinary Practice

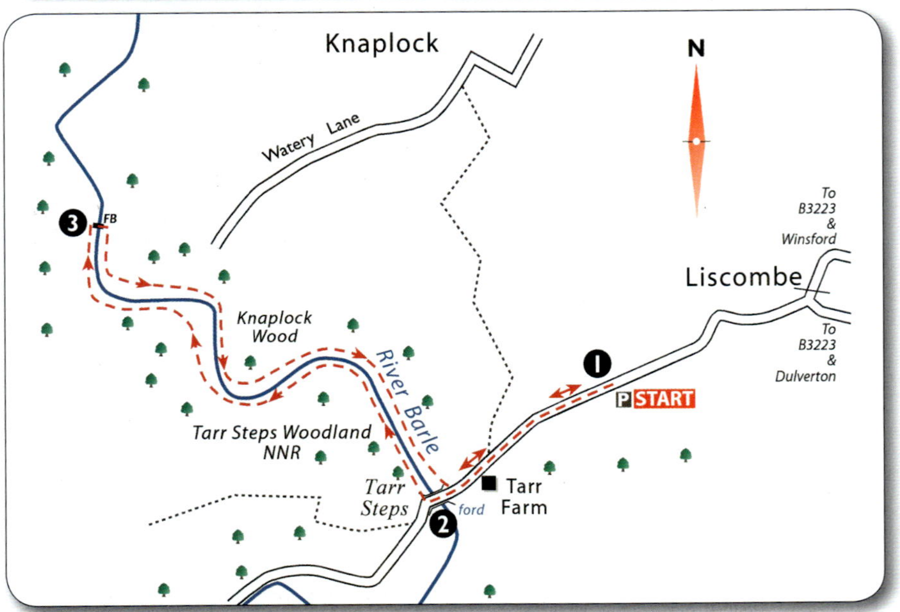

for Tarr Steps. Pass through the hamlet of Liscombe and continue following the signs for Tarr Steps. As you descend a hill, you will see a large car park on your left-hand side. There is no parking beyond this point.

Nearest refreshments

The Tarr Farm Inn dates back to the 16th century and tastefully combines pub and tea gardens. It is set high on a bank overlooking the ancient Tarr Steps and ample seating can be found both inside and out. Soup, sandwiches, ploughman's, cream teas, cakes, speciality teas and a variety of hot meals are available during the day with a full à la carte menu in the evening. Open all year from 11 am to 5.30 pm. When the tea gardens close, the inn reopens at 7.30 pm for dinner. ☎ 01643 851507.

Tarr Farm Inn, adjacent to the Tarr Steps.

The Walk

1 Leave the car park at the bottom end and follow the footpath down to where **Tarr Steps** cross the river. Go over the clapper bridge.

2 Turn right to follow the river upstream, keeping it on your right-hand side. In about ¾ mile, after using stepping stones to cross a ford, you come to a footbridge across the **River Barle**.

As you pass along this section, watch out for what appears to be an inadequate wire-rope bridge across the river. Closer inspection will show that, in fact, this is a tree-catcher. After heavy rainfall, a deluge of floodwater can rush as a torrent down this valley, sweeping away trees in its path. The tree-catcher is there to protect the ancient bridge from damage from such flood debris.

3 Turn right to cross the bridge. Turn right again to follow the river bank all the way back to **Tarr Steps**.

On your return leg, watch out for an old tree trunk that has fallen alongside the track. Look closely and you will see that hundreds, if not thousands, of copper coins have been hammered into its trunk. I have yet to discover why!

Horner Water

The view from Windsor Walk.

This is a glorious route through dense ancient woods, providing a cacophony of bird song in the spring, the chance to hear the rutting red deer stags in October and an abundance of squirrels to keep dogs well alert. The first section of the walk, which starts at Horner, nestling beneath Webber's Post and Dunkery Beacon, passes over a packhorse bridge to gently ascend through deciduous woodland. The return leg passes along 'Windsor Walk', with stunning views towards the Atlantic Ocean. This is one of the many 'walks' named by the Acland family who once owned the Holnicote Estate. It is typical of many such bridleways which run along the contour lines of a valley side, and which were designed to take advantage of the splendid views.

As you pass along Horner Water, watch out for grey wagtails (yellow and grey) and even the elusive dipper, a small bird which feeds along the rocky bottom of the river. Leaving the car park by the footpath in the corner by

Dog factors

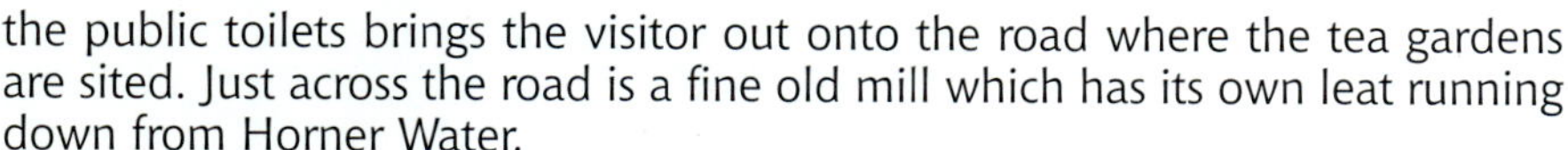

Distance: 3½ miles.
Road walking: 200 yards in Horner.
Livestock: None.
Stiles: None.
Nearest vets: White Lodge Veterinary Clinic, Minehead .

the public toilets brings the visitor out onto the road where the tea gardens are sited. Just across the road is a fine old mill which has its own leat running down from Horner Water.

Terrain

Mostly broad paths, which can be stony in places, passing through steep-sided wooded combes. The outgoing leg follows Horner Water gently uphill and this is wonderful countryside in which the dogs can run free. Firm underfoot pretty well in all weathers.

Where to park

The free public car park near the Horner Tea Gardens (GR 898454). The car park also has toilet facilities. **OS map**: Explorer OL9 Exmoor.

How to get there

Travelling between Minehead and Porlock on the A39, Horner is signposted to the south about ¾ mile outside Porlock. Follow the road, which soon leads you past the caravan park, into Horner village where the car park is well signposted and easy to find on your left-hand side.

Nearest refreshments

The tea gardens at Horner lie adjacent to the car park, alongside the fast flowing Horner Water. The gardens can seat over a hundred and a veranda offers some cover in poor weather. There are wonderful views up into the valley. As well as cream teas, a range of snacks is available such as ploughman's, jacket potatoes, sandwiches and cakes. Open daily from 11 am to 5 pm from the nearest Saturday to 25th March to the end of September. The gardens are also open between Lady Day and Easter then in October from 11.30 am to 5 pm. To confirm opening times at the margins of the holiday season, ☎ 01643 862380.

Out of season, when the tea rooms are closed, a warm welcome is given to dogs at the Royal Oak in the centre of Porlock village. This is an excellent inn providing not just good quality food for dog owners but, frequently, doggy chews for their canine companions. ☎ 01643 862798.

The Walk

1 Exit the car park by going past the toilet block to reach the road. Turn right onto the road and as it bears around to the right, take the track on the left, signposted to **Horner Wood**, just before a small stream. Go over a bridge then bear left to take the right-hand of two gates before you. Go past a field on your left to join again with **Horner Water**. Continue uphill, with the river on your left, going past a footbridge, until reaching a signpost for '**Dunkery Beacon**' pointing to a route over another footbridge across the river. Ignore this one as well and continue on upstream for 80 yards.

The path along Windsor Walk.

2 Fork left to continue your riverside walk, now with **West Water** on your left-hand side. In about ½ mile your path rejoins the main track at a point where a signpost points back to the right and where you will see a footbridge on your left which crosses over **West Water**.

3 Turn right to head back along the wide, broad track, returning to the footbridge at the end of point 2 on your outward leg. Turn right over the bridge and continue straight ahead and uphill, following a stream which is on your left. Cross the stream on a footbridge and bear slightly right where in a few yards you will see a signpost pointing left to **Windsor Walk**.

4 Turn left onto **Windsor Walk** and continue gently uphill with **Horner Water** below on your left. A track merges in from behind on your right just before a fork in the track. Take the right-hand track, heading uphill and going past a couple of bench seats. These both provide wonderful views but the second is best with stunning views to the Channel. About 20 yards after the second bench,

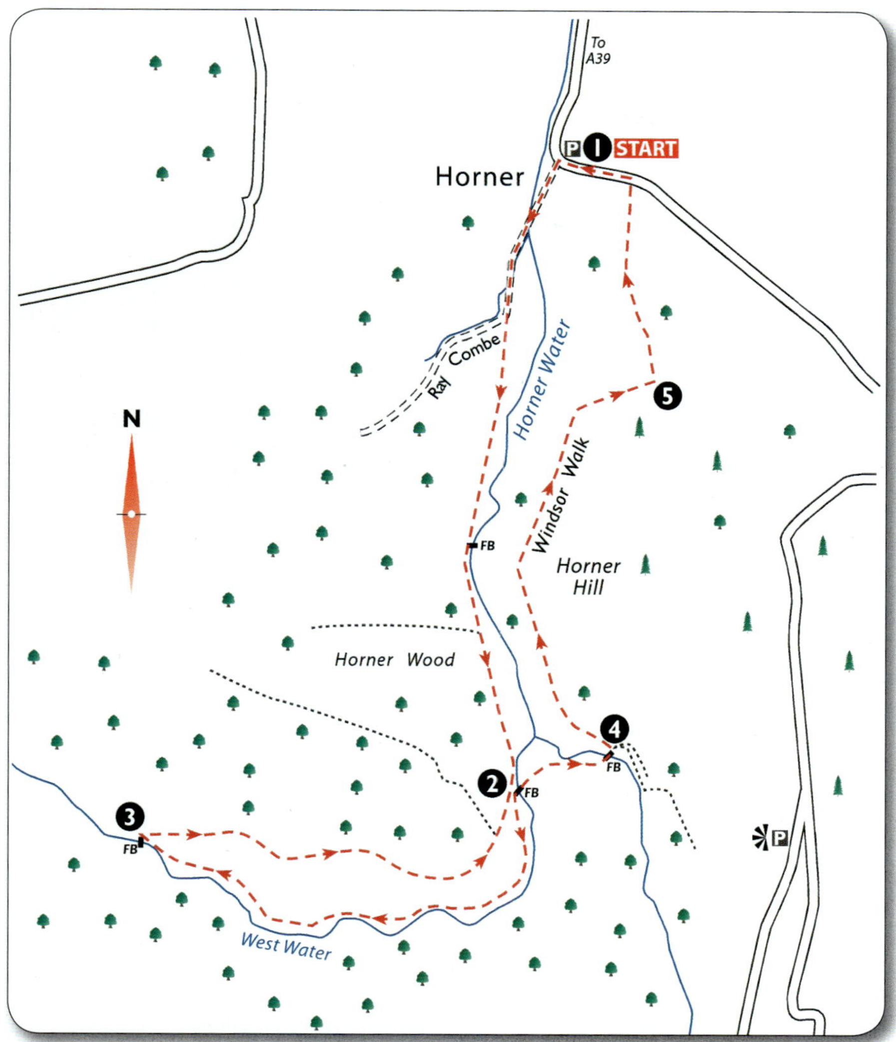

a track joins from the right. Continue straight ahead, signposted to **Horner**. In a few yards, a broader track crosses yours with a large deer gate on your left.

⑤ Turn left through the deer gate and follow the track all the way downhill to the metalled road. Turn left on the road and in 100 yards you will reach the tea gardens and the entrance to the car park.

Haddon Hill & Bury

The packhorse bridge at Bury.

This is a very pleasant excursion amidst some of Exmoor's finest scenery, with fine views over Wimbleball Lake, one of Somerset's largest man-made reservoirs. Dogs and their owners will all enjoy this circuit, which has plenty of riverside and woodland walking. Well-controlled dogs can run safely in the woods and there is rarely livestock on the open moorland.

Terrain

Mostly riverside stony tracks and woodland walking. Parts can be sticky after rain. One moderate uphill ascent at the start of the return leg. This is a good route for a hot, dry day when the walking will be firmer underfoot and when there is plenty of shade to be found in the wooded areas, especially along the river at the start.

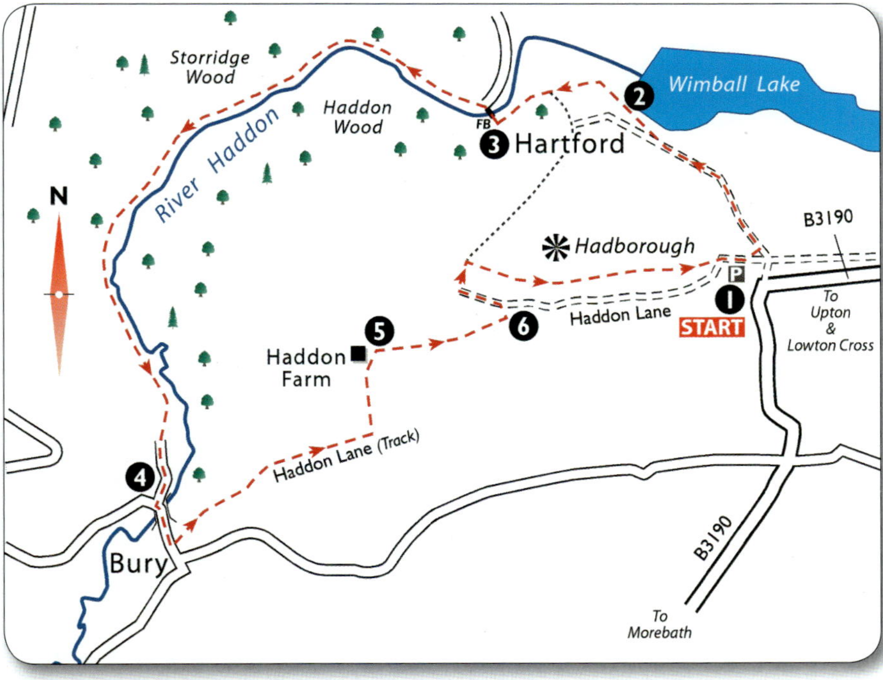

Where to park

The free public car park (which has toilet facilities) on Haddon Hill (GR 970284). **OS map:** Explorer OL9 Exmoor.

How to get there

Haddon Hill is on the B3190 between Bampton to the south and Watchet to the north, halfway between the hamlets of Morebath and Upton, about 1¼ miles from each village. The car park will be found at the peak of the high ground overlooking Wimbleball Lake, on a right-angled bend in the road.

Dog factors

Distance: 5½ miles.
Road walking: 400 yards of very quiet unclassified road.
Livestock: None.
Stiles: None.
Nearest vets: White Lodge Veterinary Clinic, Minehead.

Nearest refreshments

The 16th-century Lowtrow Cross Inn, about a mile east of Upton. The good food served here makes the inn very popular with the locals. Standing by the crossroads on the B3190, it will be found just a couple of miles east of your starting point. Although dogs are not allowed inside, there are wooden tables in the garden area, which is really pleasant when the weather is fine. ☎ 01398 371220.

The Walk

1 Leave the car park by passing through a kissing gate alongside the interpretation panel. Turn right onto a track to reach a metalled service road. Turn left onto this very quiet road and follow it downhill all the way to the dam at **Wimbleball Lake.**

Before continuing ahead, you may like to take a diversion across the top of the dam to enjoy the views across the lake. Notice what appears to be a very steep flight of steps on the lower side of the dam. This is the salmon leap, which allows spawning salmon to make their way up over the dam.

2 At the dam, continue straight ahead, signposted '**Bury** 2½ miles', to go down a metalled road. By ignoring any side routes you travel along **Lady Harriet's Drive**. At the bottom of the track, after passing through a gate, as you approach a bridge, bear left onto a green track signposted 'Bridleway to **Bury**' to reach a ford. Turn right over the river using the footbridge, signposted as the footpath, and then bear left to follow the river, now on the other side.

3 Follow the path as it leads you between the houses to follow a track to your left signposted '**Bury** 2½ miles'. Continue along this mostly stony track as it hugs the river bank all the way to **Bury**, just before which the track becomes a metalled road as you approach a T-junction.

4 Turn left to cross the packhorse bridge over the river. Ignore the track to the left which follows the river up the other bank and continue straight ahead, on the metalled road, uphill for about 80 yards, eventually turning left between houses onto a bridleway signposted to **Haddon Hill**. This is just before the red telephone box. Follow this deeply sunken track as it heads steeply uphill. In just over ½ mile, the track bears to the left at a right-angle, still continuing uphill towards **Haddon Farm**.

5 Passing to the left of the farm, pick up the farm access track as it turns right into a sunken lane. Continue ahead, ignoring a track that drops down to the

right, to reach the woodland. Continue along the obvious track through the trees, passing a stile on your left.

6 Shortly after the stile, a track doubles back on your left to a gate in just a few yards. Follow the track as it bears left, ignoring a track that goes off to your right through a gate. In 200 yards pass through a gate, bearing right to almost immediately face a fork. Take either path uphill and you will soon reach a significant track crossing yours. Turn right onto that track, which leads all the way back to your car park.

The Ordnance Survey map will give you the impression that you should be walking along a woodland edge on this final section when clearly you are not. Fear not, the wood was felled some while ago and very few visible signs linger.

Wimbleball Lake viewed from the car park.

East Quantoxhead & Kilve Beach

The duck pond at East Quantoxhead.

This is a fairly level and rectangular walk using tracks across arable land and a coastal path. The route drops down to the coastline at Kilve Beach, where a large freshwater pool provides an excellent opportunity for water-loving dogs to cool off with a swim. It is also a particularly nice spot to stop for a picnic. Halfway round the walk there is an option to cut it short if you spent too much time on the beach. Apart from Kilve Beach, the rest of the coastal section is on cliff tops, along most of which fencing or brambles prevent access to the cliff itself. However, there are areas where you may prefer to keep your dog on the lead especially if it is of a more adventurous nature.

Dog factors

Distance: 3 miles.
Road walking: 200 yards of quiet lane.
Livestock: None usually but there is the possibility of sheep between points 1 and 2; also between 7 and 1. There may be cattle between points 5 and 6.
Stiles: None.
Nearest vets: Quantock Veterinary Hospital, Nether Stowey.

Terrain

Easy to follow and mostly level tracks, with one short but gradual uphill climb. Almost the entire route offers views across the Bristol Channel to South Wales and up to the Mendip Hills.

Where to park

The village car park by East Quantoxhead church (GR 137435). You will find a donation box at the exit. There is alternative pay and display parking and start point at Kilve Beach (between points 2 and 3 on the route – GR 144442). **OS map:** Explorer 140 Quantock Hills & Bridgwater.

How to get there

From the A39 between Williton and Nether Stowey, take the signposted road to East Quantoxhead. Follow this to the end where the car park will be on the left as you come to the duck pond on the right. This will not be your road back to the A39 since the visibility at the road junction is almost non-existent. Instead, on your return, shortly after leaving the car park, there are two roads that lead to the main road. Take the signposted route to the right where the visibility is much better on reaching the main road.

Nearest refreshments

During the summer months a tea room operates in East Quantoxhead and is signposted from the car park.

The Chantry Tea Gardens at Kilve are on the route and offer cream teas, sandwiches, light lunches, ploughman's, cold meats, quiches and soups. Everything is home made except the bread, which is baked locally. Open all year except Christmas from 10 am to 5.30 pm. ☎ 01278 741457.

The 16th-century Plough Inn at Holford, south-east of Kilve, is full of old world charm and offers an excellent selection of meals and real ales. Well-behaved dogs are welcome in the walled outside seating area, albeit alongside the main A39. ☎ 01278 741232.

Kilve beach – a fossil hunter's paradise.

The Walk

. . . .

1 Leaving the car park, turn right and then left to pass around the far side of the duck pond. Follow the path past the cottage on your left to reach a choice of gates. The one to the left leads straight down to the coast and is the track that provides a route back if you wish to cut the walk short. Take the gate to the right which heads across the fields and is signposted to **Kilve church**, keeping the woodland on your right-hand side for the first section.

There is an entrance into the woodland, which provides an opportunity for energetic dogs to let off some steam if required. A circular route brings you back to the same gate.

Continue through three fields and cross a bridged stream to reach a tarred road at **Kilve** by the **Chantry Tea Gardens**.

2 Turn left onto the road, which leads down to the coast, passing to the left of the derelict brick-built oil retort, which stands before you. Go through a gate and follow the tarmac path for a short distance to reach the shoreline.

This brick and cast-iron retort is all that survives of a failed attempt in the 1920s by the Shaline Company to turn Kilve into the oil producing centre of the South West. In 1916 it was discovered that the cliffs contained bituminous Liassic shale potentially capable of yielding oil. Trials proved the venture to be too costly to justify the low yield achievable and the retort survives as a relic.

This stretch of the shore is particularly rich in fossils, especially after storms, and is frequently visited by college and university groups. At the beach, on your right there is a small pond fed by fresh running water where my dog always likes to take a swim before continuing the walk.

3 On reaching the shore, turn left and ascend the short uphill path along the cliff top to pass through a waymarked field gate. Follow the cliff top path for the full length of the field to your left. You will come to a small, dry creek around which the coastal path skirts. Here concrete steps lead down to the beach, which you may like to take in as a detour. Turn left at the dry creek to head inland, with the splendid **Court House** standing before you to your right. In a few yards you reach a footpath signpost where you may now take the short cut back to the car park (follow 4a) or complete the full route (follow 4b).

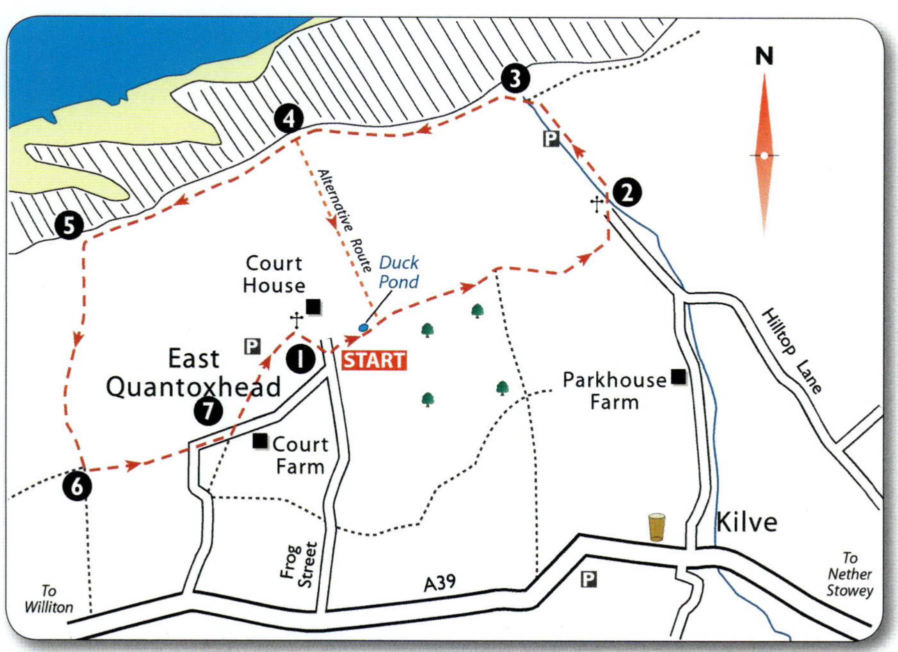

4 (a) Follow the signposted path ('**East Quantoxhead**') heading inland between two wire fences, towards the large woodland. After passing through two kissing gates, turn right at the T-junction of paths signposted to **East Quantoxhead** to reach the car park.

4 (b) Turn right onto the signposted permissive footpath and pass through a kissing gate to continue along the coastline.

Energetic dogs should be on the lead for a short section along here with cliffs to your right. Ahead of you and projecting into the sea is North Hill, which stands high over Minehead. Across the Channel is the coastline of South Wales.

Follow this path to reach another kissing gate, which leads into a field.

5 Turn left here and follow the left-hand field boundary across three fields to reach a stone and dirt lane.

6 Turn left onto the lane and follow it to its end where it meets the metalled road. Turn left onto the road.

7 In 200 yards turn left through a seven-bar field gate to follow the signposted footpath to a similar gate on the far side and in line with the church. Pass through that gate and bear right to go through a kissing gate in front of a long line of old stables to reach the car park.

Cockercombe

Aisholt village viewed from the common.

This is a circuit through woodland. It starts uphill through trees and a forest glade, then is fairly level through woods and open moorland on the middle section before the final downhill stretch passing through Cockercombe Bottom where the autumn colours can be quite stunning. Squirrels abound here and offer plenty of trails for dogs to follow. The autumn also provides an abundance of pheasants. Expect to see buzzards, jays, woodpeckers, red deer and, if you're very lucky, you may spot a dipper or two in the stream along Cockercombe Bottom.

Dog factors

Distance: 3½ miles.
Road walking: 50 yards on a quiet unclassified road.
Livestock: None.
Stiles: None.
Nearest vets: Quantock Veterinary Hospital, Nether Stowey.

Terrain

Mostly wide, well-maintained forestry tracks. Well suited to wet weather; only the first ¼ mile is prone to sticky conditions, otherwise firm underfoot. The entire walk is on forestry roads except the last 50 yards, which are on a single-track unclassified road. This is a working forest and at times timber felling will take place. In such exceptional cases, the foresters provide notices to indicate the areas in which felling is being carried out and may tape off sections where the public are temporarily excluded.

Where to park

The forestry hut in Cockercombe (GR 187365). **OS map:** Explorer 140 Quantock Hills & Bridgwater.

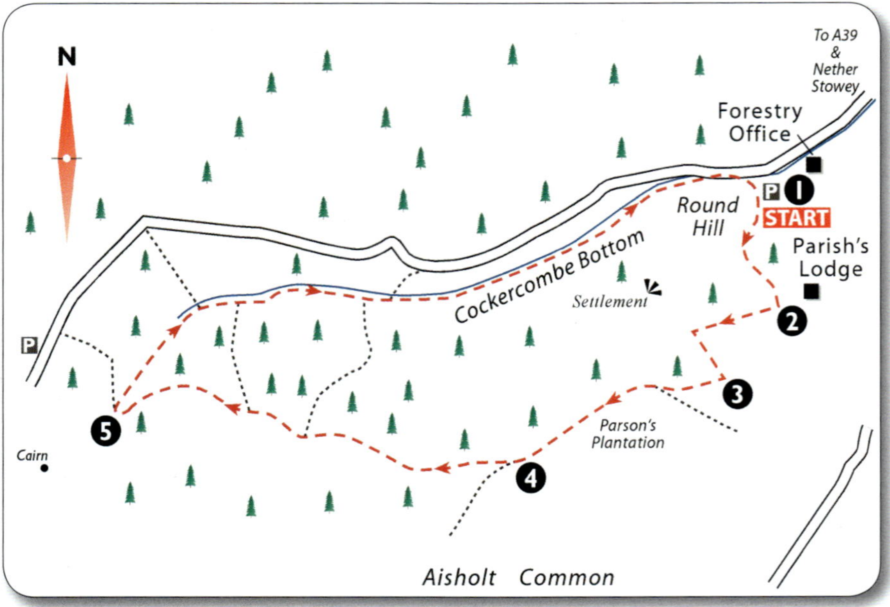

On Aisholt common.

How to get there

Turn southwards off the A39 between Cannington and Nether Stowey by the Cottage Inn at Keenthorne, signposted to Over Stowey. At the second crossroads, turn left, signposted to Aisholt. Take the first turning right, signposted to Cockercombe and Triscombe. In ½ mile, just after a cattle grid, the parking area will be found to your left by the large forestry hut.

Nearest refreshments

The Ancient Mariner is a well-frequented inn in nearby Nether Stowey (2 miles), which serves excellent food and welcomes dogs as well as their owners in the bar. It takes its name from the poem by Samuel Taylor Coleridge whose one-time home is just across the road and in the ownership of the National Trust. ☎ (inn): 01278 733544.

The Walk

1 From the car park, with your back to the road, take the path past the single-bar forestry gate, which heads uphill into the woods. Follow the obvious uphill track, ignoring a track leading off to the left, to reach an open glade. Through the trees to your left is the isolated property known as **Parish's**.

2 Once into the clearing, bear right to follow the right-hand side of the glade, leaving it on an obvious track back into the woodland. Follow this uphill to a significant crossroads of tracks. At this point you will be able to see the skyline through the lower part of the trees ahead. Turn left here to follow the path between deciduous trees to reach a T-junction with a forestry gate to your left. Before you are open fields with a fine view down over the village of **Aisholt**, the one-time home of the poet, Sir Henry Newbolt, with its towered church.

3 Turn right at the T-junction to follow the now fairly level track, with forest to your right and a fence to your left. Continue until just past the brow of the hill where a wide path joins from the right-hand side and a gate is found to your left. Continue straight ahead here for 40 yards to where the path splits.

4 The left-hand path follows the fence but you need to bear right, sticking to the more obvious forestry road. Continue straight ahead to pass a wide open space to your right at the head of a combe which drops down to your right. Continue on the same main forestry track as it drops rapidly down with the valley of **Cockercombe** on your right-hand side. The path at the bottom of that combe is your return route.

5 Just after the track levels out, it swings sharp right as it crosses a deep-cleft gully that runs down into **Cockercombe**. Immediately after the gully, the path splits with the main track continuing uphill to the left, but here you take the lesser track heading downhill to the right and signposted into **Cockercombe Bottom**. Now just stay on the track all the way down the combe, following the stream as it leads you back to the car park with just the last 50 yards being on a quiet road.

Lydeard Hill

Buster at Wills Neck – the highest point on the Quantocks.

Two triangular circuits make up this 4-mile walk. It is mostly fairly level across woodland-lined, open moorland and, in the middle section, takes in Wills Neck, the highest point on the Quantock Hills, affording magnificent views. Red deer can often be spotted but generally on the far side of the combes which you will be skirting. The free-roaming hill ponies frequent this area and peregrine falcons may be seen in the vicinity of Triscombe Quarry. The whole of this walk is on open moorland where well-behaved dogs can run freely and the views are splendid throughout.

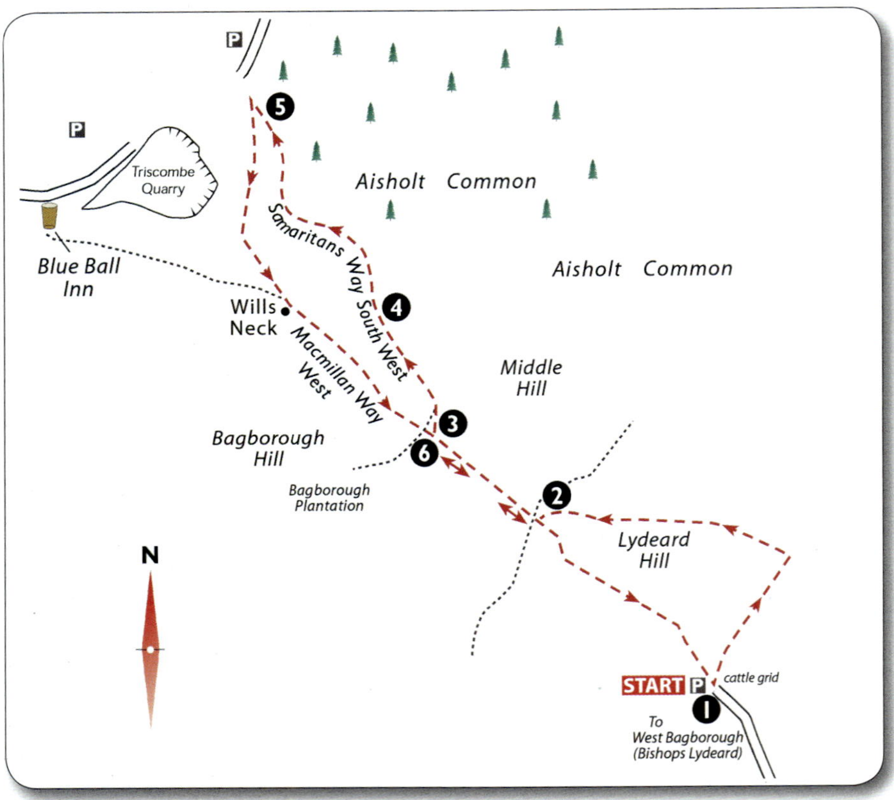

Dog factors

Distance: 4 miles.
Road walking: None.
Livestock: Possibility of free-roaming moorland sheep and ponies.
Stiles: None.
Nearest vets: Quantock Veterinary Hospital, Nether Stowey.
Quarry: There is a deep quarry about 100 yards from the route (point 5). This is referred to in the walk instructions. A good fence runs all the way around the top of the quarry but there is also the possibility of pheasants. Owners of springer spaniels may like to put their dogs on a lead for about 100 yards until past this section, unless their dogs are fitted with parachutes! It's a very deep drop.

Terrain

Mostly firm bridleway with one stony and gullied stretch. Well suited to wet weather. Where damp sections exist, there is always a nearby alternative track running in parallel.

Where to park

Lydeard Hill car park (GR 180338). **OS map:** Explorer 140 Quantock Hills & Bridgwater.

How to get there

From the B-road between Enmore (west of Bridgwater) and Bishops Lydeard, take the side road signposted as 'West Bagborough 1¼'. In ⅓ mile turn right, signposted 'Lydeard Hill car park ¼', onto a no-through road at the end of which, after a cattle grid, you will see the car park.

Nearest refreshments

The Pines Café on Buncombe Hill, Broomfield is open all year round and serves hot and cold snack-type lunches and teas. There is ample outdoor seating outside where dogs are welcome and a large lawn area. A dog's water bowl is normally at the entrance to the café. The Pines will be found on the road between Bishops Lydeard and Enmore, at the junction with the road to Kingston St Mary and Broomfield (GR 207329). ☎ 01823 451245.

The Rising Sun will be found in the centre of nearby West Bagborough village. It is a 16th-century inn renowned for the quality of its food. Well-behaved dogs are welcome in the bar area. ☎ 01823 432575.

The Walk

• •

1 From the car park, you will see a double and adjacent single gate leading onto the moor. This will be your route back. For now, look to the right to find a kissing gate. Pass through this and follow the fence line with moorland to your left and woodland to your right. Stay on this track until you reach a fenced field boundary, turning left before the fence to follow a bridleway with the fence on your right-hand side. When the fence line turns away to your right, continue straight ahead along the obvious bridleway with views across to **Aisholt Common** on your right (there is the possibility of sighting red deer). Ignore the path that heads off to your left and continue ahead on the obvious track towards the woodland ahead. The track swings left just before the wood to reach a gate and stile.

2 Pass through the gate and continue along the wide dirt track with woodland on your left. In ¼ mile you reach a fork with a post ('No bikes – No vehicles') in the middle with a yellow arrow pointing straight ahead, which will be your return route.

3 Turn right at the post onto a stony track with a valley dropping away to your right. The path swings left and then right to reach a point where a path merges from behind you to your left. In front of you the path splits.

4 Take the narrower, stony and gullied track on the left to reach the woodland edge where you bear left onto an adjoining track, keeping the main woodland's fence on your right-hand side. Follow this beech-tree-lined track all the way to 30 yards before a metal gate.

On the outward route.

5 Turn diagonally back to your left to follow an uphill track. Stay on this as it sweeps left and uphill to a ridge.

NB: to your right you will see a fence that runs around the top of a very deep quarry with sheer drops over the edge. Notices along the quarry warn of the dangers. You will not be able to see the quarry unless you approach it and peer over. The fence should be high enough to keep most dogs out but we all know what springer spaniels are capable of. You may want to secure your dogs until reaching the ridge of the hill.

On reaching the ridge, you will see the triangulation point at **Wills Neck**, the highest point on the **Quantocks**. After stopping to enjoy the views, continue in the same direction along a broad track towards the woodland. On reaching the trees, keep the main wooded area on your right and continue straight ahead on the bold track until you reach the post mentioned at point 3 on your outward journey.

6 Continue straight ahead here with the valley dropping away to your left. Retrace your steps to the gate at point 2. At the gate, take the right-hand gravelled track with a fence on the right and follow the fence line all the way back to the car park.

Taunton Canal & River

The resident swan on the bank of the River Tone.

This absolutely level route provides an opportunity for dog walkers to taste the countryside in the very middle of the county town. It is made up entirely of riverside and canal path walking, where well-behaved dogs can run free, with just the short section between points 4 and 5 requiring leads. Kingfishers may be seen along the stretch through the 'Children's Wood' where rabbits are always in abundance.

Terrain

Mostly gravel or grit pathways and well suited to wet weather. Apart from crossing the odd bridge, there are no inclines.

The weir on the River Tone at Firepool Lock.

Dog factors

Distance: 3 miles.
Road walking: One short stretch of about 200 yards (point 4).
Livestock: None.
Stiles: One token stile – very low at about 1 ft high. Step over – not climb over.
Nearest vets: Neil Rudram Ltd, Taunton.
Railway crossing: There is one point on this walk where the mainline railway is to be crossed. It is an unmanned 'Stop – Look – Listen' crossing with good visibility over a long distance in both directions.

Where to park

The pay and display Coal Orchard car park at the Brewhouse Theatre site (GR 227248). **OS map:** Explorer 128 Taunton & Blackdown Hills.

How to get there

From the M5 Junction 25, head into Taunton along the dual carriageway. Go straight across at the two roundabouts. At a third is a petrol filling station. Your road goes just to the left of the mini-roundabout into St James Street. Turn right at the Ring of Bells pub and then left into the Coal Orchard car park. This is your start point.

Nearest refreshments

The Boathouse, just beyond point 2 on the route, is a light and airy riverside café, very pleasantly situated. Instead of turning right over the bridge, continue on towards the next bridge and you will see it on your left. Seating is available inside and out, and dogs are welcome outside. There is a range of hot and cold meals and drinks, including daily specials and locally-made cakes. Open Monday to Saturday 9 am to 5 pm; Sunday 10 am to 4 pm, ☎ 01823 352033.

The Walk

1 On the far side of the car park you will find a riverside pathway. Turn right at the path to follow the riverside walk with the **River Tone** on your left-hand side. You will reach a footbridge with a 'Pluto' sign at its entrance. The Morrisons' supermarket is on the opposite bank.

2 Cross the footbridge and turn right to follow the riverside path, keeping the river on your right-hand side. Pass under a road bridge and then a footbridge before reaching **Firepool Lock**. This is the point where the **Bridgwater and Taunton Canal** links to the **River Tone**.

3 On reaching a tarred path, turn right (signposted 'National Cycle Network 3 – **Bridgwater** and **Creech St Michael**') to cross over the canal bridge and then go immediately left to follow the canal path with the canal on your left-hand side and the river on your right. Stay on the towpath to pass under a footbridge, a railway bridge, a large road bridge and then a small road bridge.

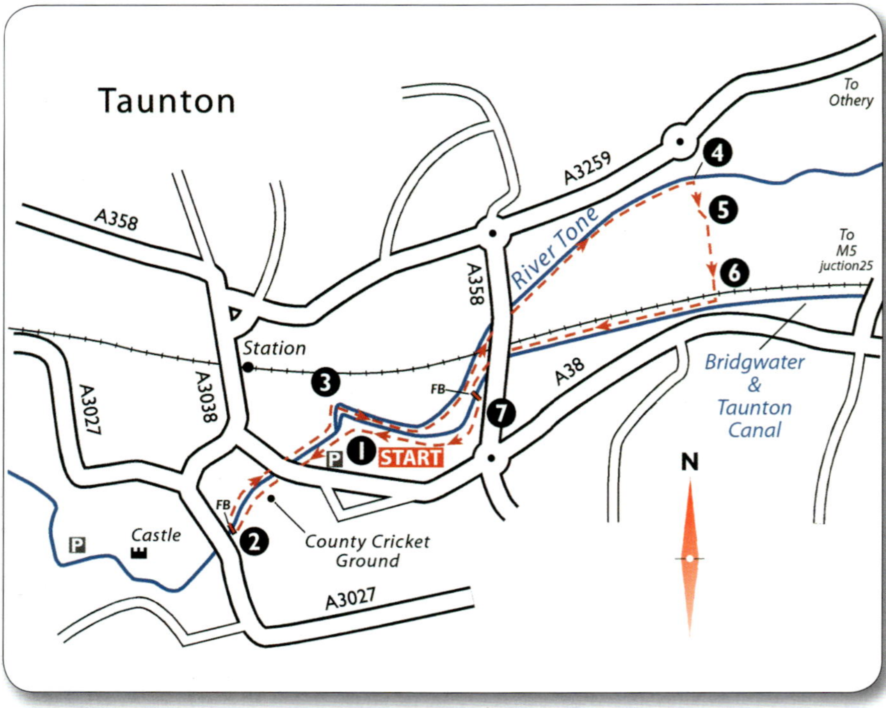

Somerset - A Dog Walker's Guide

4 At the next road bridge, go up to the busy road (dogs on leads along here for about 200 yards). Turn right onto the road and follow it as it bears left.

5 Shortly after it bears left, look for a low-down stile on the right-hand side, only about a foot high. Pass through this onto a track which leads to the railway line.

   Caution – this is the main Exeter to Bristol line but visibility is excellent in both directions. It is an unmanned 'Stop – Look – Listen' crossing.

6 Once across the railway line, you enter the '**Children's Wood**', a riverside walkway where between 1992 and 1995 one tree was planted for each child born in Taunton. Turn right here to follow the pleasant riverside path, passing under a road bridge to reach a footbridge across the river.

7 Cross the bridge and immediately turn right to follow the riverside walk back to your car park.

Prior's Park Wood

In Prior's Park Wood.

If you enjoy the aroma of garlic, then this is the walk for you on a late spring day when sections of this route are carpeted with wall-to-wall white-flowered wild garlic, occasionally giving way to blankets of bluebells. On the other hand, this is also a good circuit for one of those hot days when you can take advantage of the cooler air in the shade of the trees as you walk through the densely wooded Prior's Park. It's a beautiful walk and conveniently close to the county's capital. It also provides long stretches where well-behaved dogs can run free through the woodland, crossing streams and following all the woodland scents.

Dog factors

Distance: 4 miles.
Road walking: 600 yards of quiet no through road; 400 yards of B-road.
Livestock: In one field only, after point 4, with just 50 yards between gates.
Stiles: One at very beginning of walk – passable for small to medium breeds, otherwise leap or lift over. Worth the effort once across.
Nearest vets: Neil Rudram Ltd, Taunton.

Terrain

Mostly woodland walking, along grassy and stony tracks. Can be muddy in sections after rain. Can be steep in places, with wooded slopes. Some road walking.

Where to park

The Lamb and Flag on Blagdon Hill (GR 211181). Patrons may use the inn's car park with the licensee's approval. Please park at the far end of the car park to allow access for delivery vehicles. There is also space for kerbside parking.
OS map: Explorer 128 Taunton & Blackdown Hills.

How to get there

From Taunton town centre, take the B3170 south, following signs for Corfe/ Taunton racecourse. In the village of Corfe, turn right at the White Hart Inn, heading for Pitminster. Follow this road for 1½ miles, following signs for Blagdon. At a T-junction, turn left onto Blagdon Hill and the Lamb and Flag will be found on the left.

Nearest refreshments

The Lamb and Flag Inn, dating back to 1647, serves an excellent range of food and real ales. It was once a coaching inn and it still manages to maintain that charm. There is always a warm welcome especially for walkers and their dogs, which are allowed in all areas. Food is served all day up to 9.30 pm except for Mondays when the kitchen doesn't open until 6 pm. Prior reservations are advisable at busy times. There is a beer garden with sweeping views over the Vale of Taunton. ☎ 01823 421736.

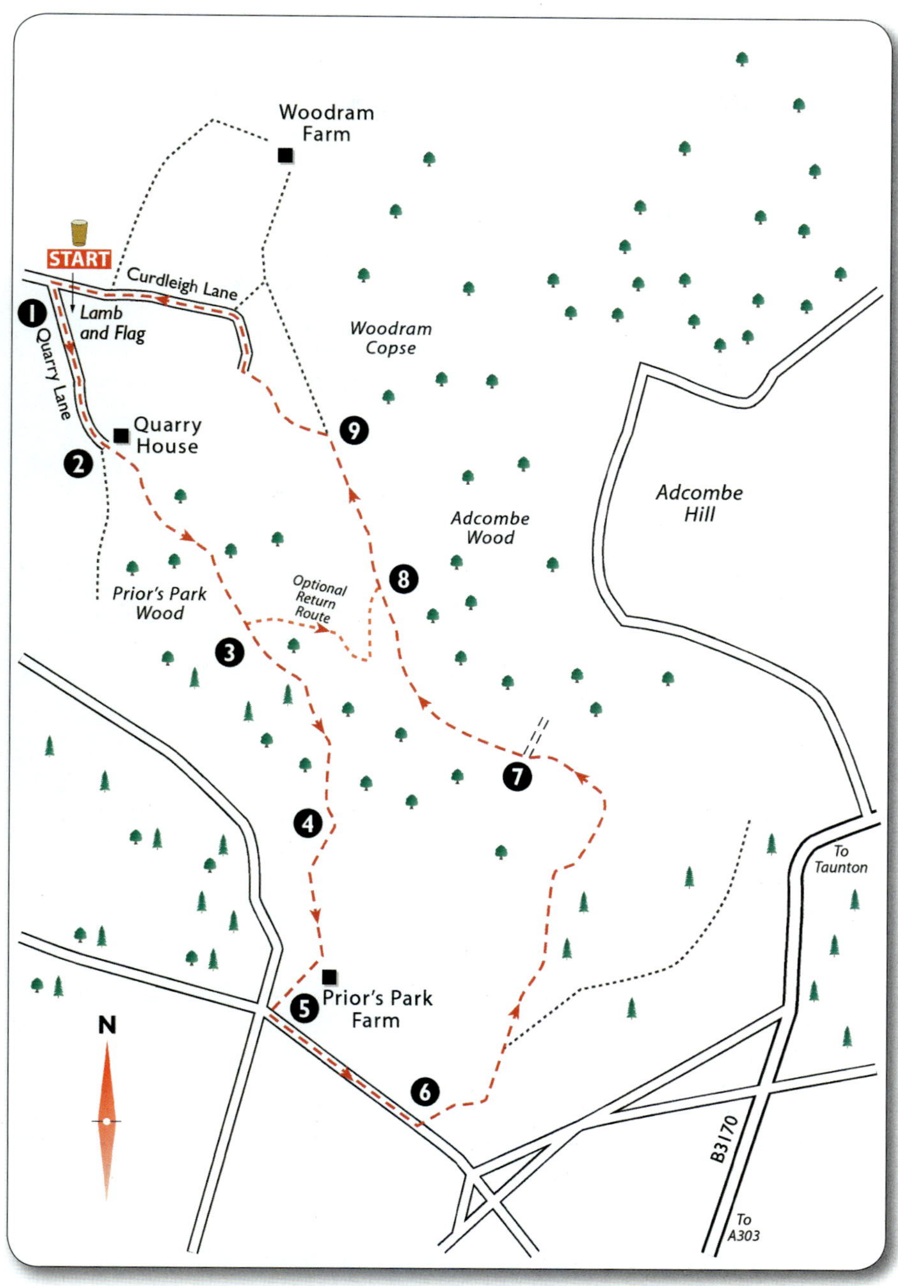

Woodram Farm
START
Curdleigh Lane
Lamb and Flag
Quarry Lane
1
Quarry House
2
Woodram Copse
9
Prior's Park Wood
Adcombe Wood
Adcombe Hill
Optional Return Route
8
3
4
7
5
Prior's Park Farm
6
To Taunton
N
B3170
To A303

The Walk

- -

1 Head east from the Lamb and Flag by going down **Curdleigh Lane,** the lane which runs alongside the pub. In about 100 yards, turn right into **Quarry Lane** at the end of which you pass between the buildings of **Quarry House** to reach a waymarked field gate.

2 Pass through the gate and continue straight ahead onto a gravelly track which takes you up into **Prior's Park Wood**.

3 In 500 yards, the main track turns left. Continue straight ahead, uphill, onto the lesser track to reach a gate leading into a field at the upper edge of the woodland. (There may be cattle in this field but it is only 50 yards to your gate out of the field.)

4 Follow the left-hand field boundary for 50 yards to reach a gate. Turn left through the gate and follow the waymarked footpath straight ahead between two lines of fences to reach **Prior's Park Farm**.

The last time I passed through I met the farm dogs, one of which is the unusual brown-coloured Australian Kelpie. This is officially described as an Australian sheepdog which excels at herding and driving cattle with little or no commands or guidance. Its owner, however, described it as totally useless except for agility work!

At the farm, turn right between the farm buildings onto the farm access road, signposted as a footpath, to reach the road.

5 At the road (dogs on lead, please – fast traffic albeit good visibility), turn left to follow the road for about 400 yards.

6 Take a track to your left leading into the forest by a stile alongside a gate. This is the only stile on the route and often the forestry gate is left open or unlocked. Just after a left-hand bend, the path splits. Take the lesser path which drops down to the left to follow a stream on your left-hand side. Cross a small stream which runs in from the right and continue ahead to cross the main stream which now runs on your right-hand side. As the track curves left, ignore the lesser track to the right, keeping the stream on your right-hand side. The path curves left again and drops down to where the path is normally under water. Pass this by taking the higher ground to the left of the flooded area. Shortly after, you reach a side-track to your right.

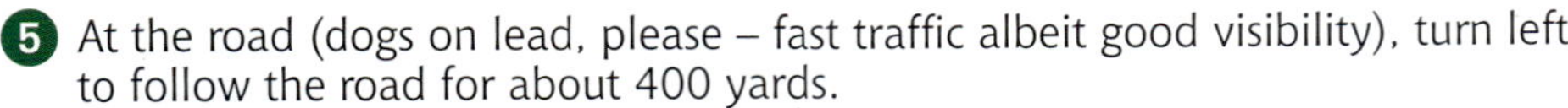
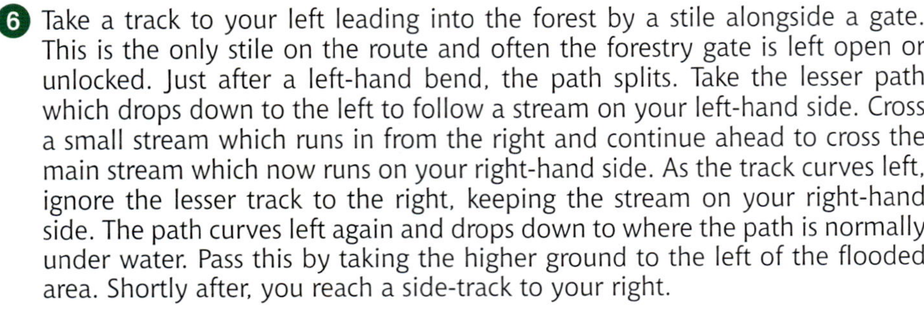

Approaching the hamlet of Curdleigh.

7 IIgnore the side track and continue straight ahead, still with the stream on your right, passing under a line of telephone wires, to reach a gated track to your left.

8 Continue straight ahead to reach a waymarked field gate just after a track merges from your right. Enter and cross the field keeping to the right-hand field boundary to reach a metalled road by a large wooden shed.

9 Turn left onto the single-track **Curdleigh Lane** and follow this all the way back to the **Lamb and Flag**.

Berrow

Berrow Sands provides plenty of space for play.

This almost level walk is in two distinct parts. The route begins and ends in the grass-covered sand-dune nature reserve at Berrow, rich in orchids in the summer months and abundant with the sound of reed and sedge warblers in the spring. The area has been designated as a Site of Special Scientific Interest (SSSI). There is rich grass on sandy soil throughout this area, ideal for rabbits, which are abundant around the dunes and hence there are plenty of foxes to feed on them. This means there are lots of 'smells' to keep dogs occupied. If you arrive in the early morning on a still day, then it

Dog factors

Distance: 1¾ miles.
Road walking: 20 yards.
Livestock: None.
Stiles: None.
Nearest vets: Smith & Partners, Berrow Road, Burnham.

can be easy to spot the footprints of the foxes in the sand: very similar to a dog's, the two front toes are much closer together and the footprints form a narrow line as though the fox were walking along a tightrope, unlike a dog's where there are two clear left and right lines.

Then there is the 'Blue Flag' beach, which is especially popular with visitors from the Midlands. It is 7 miles long in total and the section chosen for this walk provides a huge area in which to throw a ball for your dog to retrieve with no fear of it getting lost. There is also an opportunity to explore the wreck of the shipwrecked SS *Nornen*, a Norwegian barque that ran aground during a storm in 1897. Completely submerged at high tide, it provides an interesting place to explore as the tide runs out leaving salt-water pools within its skeletal hulk. The ship's crew of ten, which included a dog, were rescued by the local lifeboat and brought safely ashore at nearby Burnham.

Whilst the walk is a short one, it can be extended by several miles just by continuing to walk along the shore towards Burnham-on-Sea, at which point dogs are not allowed on the town beach, and then retracing your steps.

Terrain

Sand-dunes and open beach. The higher beach is soft underfoot but lower down provides firm walking. The tide goes out a very long way. At low tides, avoid going out too far as the mud areas develop into sinking mud/sand. It is safe to walk out as far as the shipwreck but not beyond. This still leaves a massive amount of beach to enjoy.

Where to park

The free car park on the Brean road in Berrow (GR 293536). An alternative is to use the beach car park a short distance north of the free car park. This is a

Somerset - A Dog Walker's Guide

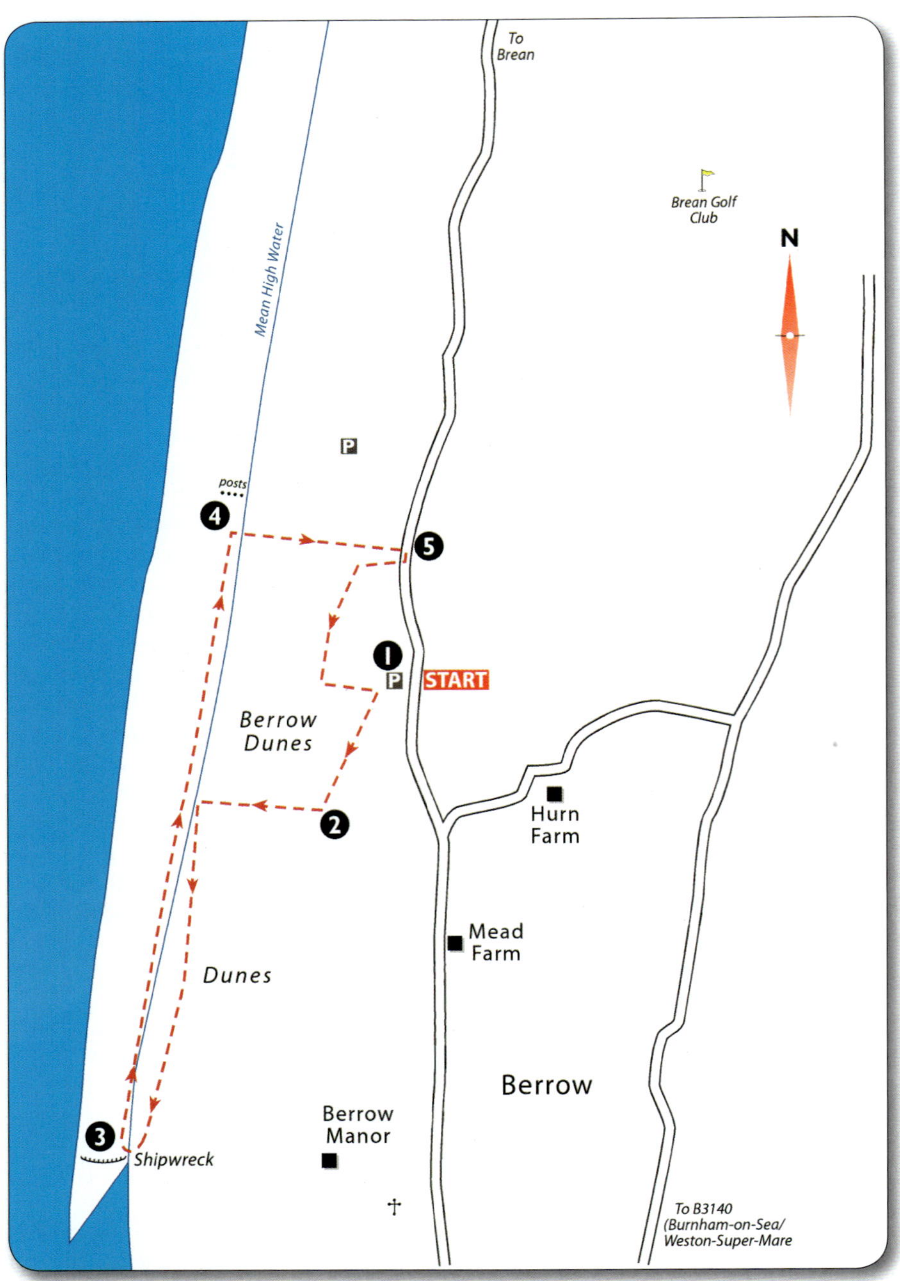

The skeletal remains of the wrecked Norwegian ship, the SS Nornen.

pay-on-entry park but allows you to leave your car on the beach. The walk can then be started at point 4. **OS map:** Explorer 153 Weston-super-Mare & Bleadon Hill.

How to get there

From Burnham-on-Sea take the B3140 north and turn off left to continue northwards towards Berrow and Brean. Once past Berrow church, shortly after a bus stop, enter the small free car park on your left-hand side, opposite the Sandy Glade Holiday Park.

Nearest refreshments

By following the B3140 north, to its very end beneath the cliffs of Brean Down, you will find the Brean Down Tropical Bird Gardens. It has its own tea rooms, which are open to the public and not just for visitors to the gardens and there is a large seated area both inside and out. The outside area provides ample table seating on a grass lawn where dogs are welcome. The menu reflects the seaside nature of this café but a cream tea can be found here, as well as a variety of hot and cold food. Open April to October, 10 am to dusk. ☎ 01278 751209.

The Walk

. . . .

1 At the left-hand end of the car park, by the nature reserve interpretation panels, turn right onto the sandy footpath and, in 80 yards, at the second white post, turn left onto a sandy track leading to a grassy downland area where rabbits' scrapes are abundant. Keep straight ahead across this area, heading for the scrubland, to reach a sandy track that crosses in front of you.

2 Turn right onto the track and follow it down to the beach. At the beach turn left and follow it for ¼ mile to discover and explore the wreck of the **SS Nornen**, as long as it's not high tide in which case it will be well submerged. From here you can extend your walk by another 2 miles (until you reach the 'No dogs' beach at **Burnham**).

3 Retrace your steps along the beach, going past the point where you joined it, and continuing past a nature reserve sign with finger-post, to approach a line of posts which runs down towards the sea in order to stop cars using sections of the beach.

4 Just before the line of posts, there is another nature reserve panel on your right-hand side. Head up and over the dunes immediately behind this panel and slightly to the right to find a well-defined track which runs along a fence line across the northern edge of the reserve to reach the road.

5 At the road, turn right and immediately right again through a gate to re-enter the reserve. Follow the gravel path straight ahead across a short grassy area to reach the top of a low ridge. Turn left once on the ridge and follow the white-topped posts marking the circular walk. On reaching a crossing of tracks, turn left, signposted to the car park. Go straight across at the next crossing of paths, heading inland, to reach your car park.

West Huntspill & Three Rivers

On the path to Maundril's Farm.

Enjoy a leisurely riverside stroll, which starts and finishes at the parish church in West Huntspill and follows the banks of three rivers, the Parrett, Brue and Huntspill. After an initial section across footpathed fields, the walk explores the muddy tidal creeks of the Bristol Estuary where 'retired' boats lie in graveyard fashion on the higher ground above those that still provide active service. It is along this stretch that well-behaved dogs can run freely, enjoying the sights and smells associated with a coastal walk. The appearance of the landscape can change dramatically as high tide replaces low, and winter waders replace summer migrants.

Dog factors

Distance: 5 miles.
Road walking: 900 yards of very quiet road.
Livestock: Cattle possible on small sections of the route but predominantly cattle free. The land is so flat here that cattle will easily be spotted well in advance of entering any fields – hence no surprises.
Stiles: 6 stiles – OK for small to medium breeds or agile larger dogs. My border collie slips easily under all of them. Larger breeds may have to jump two stiles. There are also three footbridges that are simply solid planks with a handrail.
Nearest vets: Quantock Veterinary Hospital, Bridgwater.

Terrain

Very quiet and pleasant flat walking, mostly on riverside paths. Some short stretches can be sticky after heavy rain.

Where to park

Roadside in the vicinity of St Peter's church, West Huntspill (GR 305455).
OS map: Explorer 140 Quantock Hills & Bridgwater.

How to get there

West Huntspill is reached on the A38 between Bridgwater and Highbridge. Approaching from the south, take the first turning left after crossing the Huntspill River by the Crossways Inn onto Church Road (signposted to 'Laburnum House'). From the north, turn right at the Crossways Inn. Follow this road to St Peter's church and find roadside parking where safe and practical to do so.

Nearest refreshments

The Crossways Inn on the main road welcomes dogs within the inn and offers a good range of food and drink. This 17th-century coaching house is full of charm and its menu is diverse, offering traditional pub food using locally sourced ingredients as well as a selection of more exotic dishes. ☎ 01278 783756.

The Walk

1 From the church, continue north along **Church Road**. Having passed **Cadwell's Lane** and **Plymor Road**, the road bears right and then sharply left as it passes

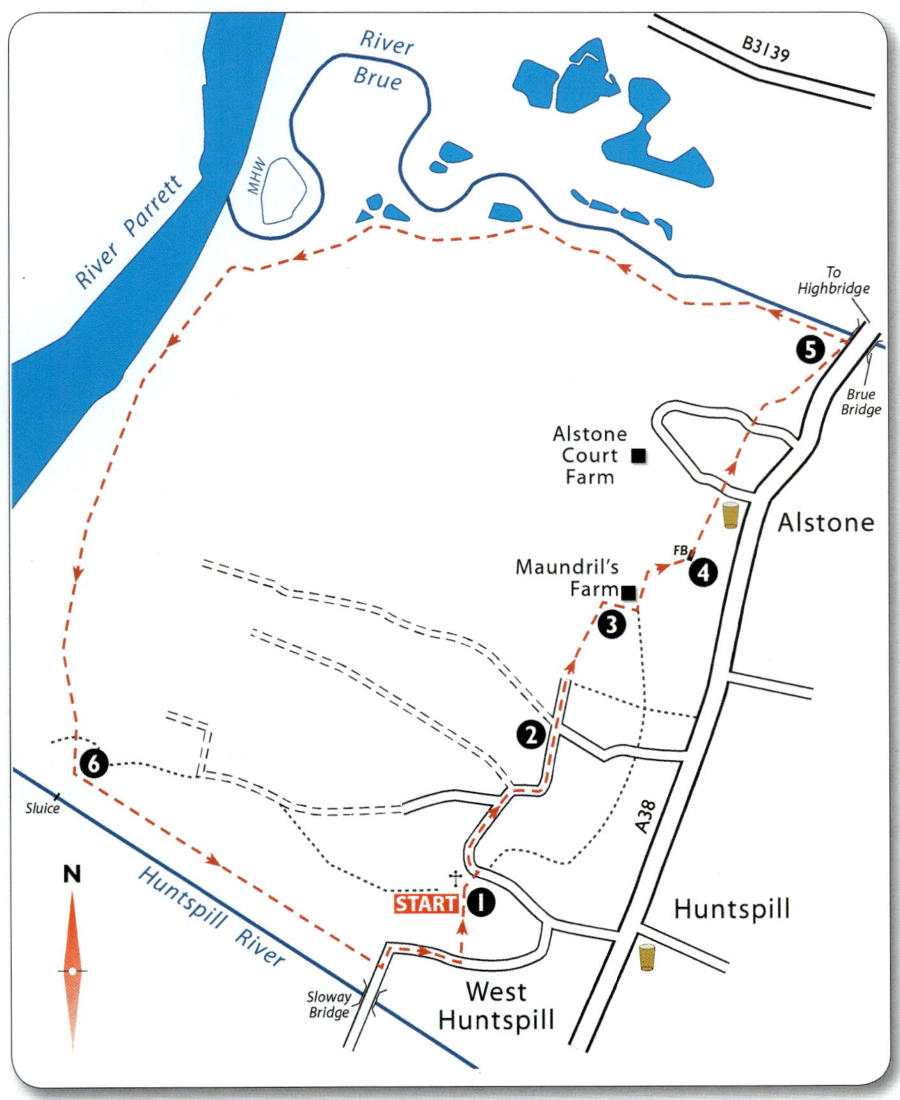

Plymor Hill Farm. About 120 yards after the sharp left bend, the road turns sharply to the right.

2 Go straight ahead at the bend, leaving **Church Road**, to enter **Langlands Lane**, which changes from metalled road to a hedge-lined green track. This links up with a concrete farm road which ends at a gate on your right leading into the farm complex over a bridge.

3 Turn right, staying on the concrete track, as indicated by the footpath signpost, to reach a group of farm buildings at **Maundril's Farm**. Turn left after the first barn to cross a signposted stile (with gate) and follow a track between the farm buildings. At the end of the buildings, go straight ahead over a concrete farm track into a green lane. At the end of the lane, enter a field and turn half right to cross the field, heading for a footbridge on the far side.

4 Cross the footbridge and follow the right-hand field boundary to a dog-friendly stile in the field corner. Go over the stile and continue along an enclosed track to reach and cross a road, continuing straight ahead onto a narrow waymarked track behind a line of bungalows. You reach and cross yet another quiet road, and, slightly to the right, keep to the same line of travel and pass between two houses to reach a field. Enter the field over the stile and follow its right-hand field boundary, crossing another stile, to reach the **River Brue**.

5 Turn left to follow the riverside, with the river on your right, to reach a set of sluices. Pass through the stile and gate to follow the raised bank of the river. In about a mile, the **River Brue** joins the **River Parrett** where three lagoons are on your right-hand side. Your path continues to curve gently to the left, heading more southward for another mile to reach the low brick buildings at the sluice where the **Huntspill River** takes its turn to join the **River Parrett**.

Along this stretch you will notice to your right the small island of Stert (home to nesting waders) and Hinkley Point Nuclear Power Station across the bay.

6 Beyond the sluice, take the service road to the left of the bank of the **Huntspill River**, using the pedestrian gate alongside the cattle grid. Now drop down off the right-hand side of the road to pick up the riverside footpath all the way to

The banks of the River Brue provide a last resting place.

reach **Sloway Bridge** and the minor road. Turn left to walk past the large hotel complex of **Laburnum House** and, ignoring the first signposted footpath to the left (which has a difficult to negotiate stile), reach a group of cottages on the right-hand side. On reaching the last cottages, look for a gap in the hedge on the opposite side. Turn left through the gap, using the footbridge and kissing gate. Go straight ahead as signposted to cross another footbridge and kissing gate, which takes you into the back of **St Peter's church**, just beyond which you return to your car.

Langport & the River Parrett

Pollarded willows along the River Parrett.

A **very level route** that follows the slow-flowing River Parrett on the outward leg and an old railway line on the return. The riverside walking is along gravelled pathways, where well-behaved dogs can run free, and then through grazing meadows along the raised river bank where discretion needs to be used if cattle are present. The railway line is grass and stone and is shared with the occasional cyclist where dogs can safely run free. It is bordered on either side with mixed hedgerow and throughout the spring abounds with the songs of the nesting birds, whitethroats, blackcaps, sedge warblers, willow warblers, chiffchaffs and a host of other delights. It also teems with butterflies, which take advantage of the proliferation of trackside herbage.

Dog factors

Distance: 4 miles.
Road walking: 200 yards of quiet road at point 3.
Livestock: Dairy cattle between points 2 and 3.
Stiles: One only and that is dog friendly.
Nearest vets: Langport Veterinary Clinic.

Terrain

Flat walking on riverside paths and old railway track. Very quiet and pleasant.

Where to park

The large free car park in the centre of Langport (GR 418267). **OS map**: Explorer 129 Yeovil & Sherborne.

How to get there

Langport is situated between Taunton and Somerton on the A378 and on the A372 which runs between Bridgwater and the A303 at Podimore. Travelling on the A372, on entering Langport, follow signs for Taunton. This will take you onto the A378, Bow Street, along which will be found the car park, well signposted on the left-hand side, opposite the large landmark clock. Approaching from Taunton, you enter Bow Street with the car park on your right. Once in the car park, head for the top-right corner of the parking area, beyond the line of shops. This gets you closest to the river bank and furthest from the shops – hence normally plenty of space.

Nearest refreshments

If you're looking to rediscover the quintessential old English pub then you could do worse than visit the Rose and Crown in Huish Episcopi, just to the east of Langport. This attractive thatched inn will be found on the A372 road to Wincanton and Yeovil, just a mile or so from Langport town centre. It is popular with walkers, and dogs on leads are given a warm welcome. When you go inside, it is like stepping back in time, into a stone-floored parlour with an old piano and framed photos of First World War soldiers. There is also ample garden space for when the weather is fine. ☎ 01458 250494.

For a closer alternative, within a few yards of the entrance to the car park, you will find the Langport Arms Hotel. Meals are served every day and dogs are welcome in the courtyard, so this is a convenient choice when the weather is fine. ☎ 01458 250520.

The Walk

. . . .

1 From the top-right corner of the car park, there is easy access onto the river bank. Turn left to walk alongside the river on your right-hand side. Follow this path for ½ mile to **Huish Bridge** where the **River Yeo** merges with the **Parrett**.

2 Cross over the bridge and turn left to follow the river bank, signposted as 'Public footpath, **Muchelney** 1m', now on the other side. Continue along the waymarked **River Parrett Trail** with the river on your left-hand side, passing through several pedestrian gates and one dog-friendly stile, to reach the road at **Westover Bridge**.

3 Turn right onto the road to reach the heavy buttresses of a one-time railway bridge, just after a lone cottage. Double-back to the right to pass through consecutive gates onto the course of the old railway line, signposted as the **Langport and Parrett Cycle Way**. Go immediately through two gates and then just follow the hedge-lined track.

4 At the far end of the track, as you approach **Langport**, pass through a gate and turn right and then left through a 'cow-crush' stile, still following the cycle trail. As you approach the main road in **Langport**, turn right between **Great Western House** and the cycle hire centre to cross a footbridge. Turn right,

On the homeward route along the River Parrett

signposted '**Huish Bridge**' to follow the river bank back to the car park.

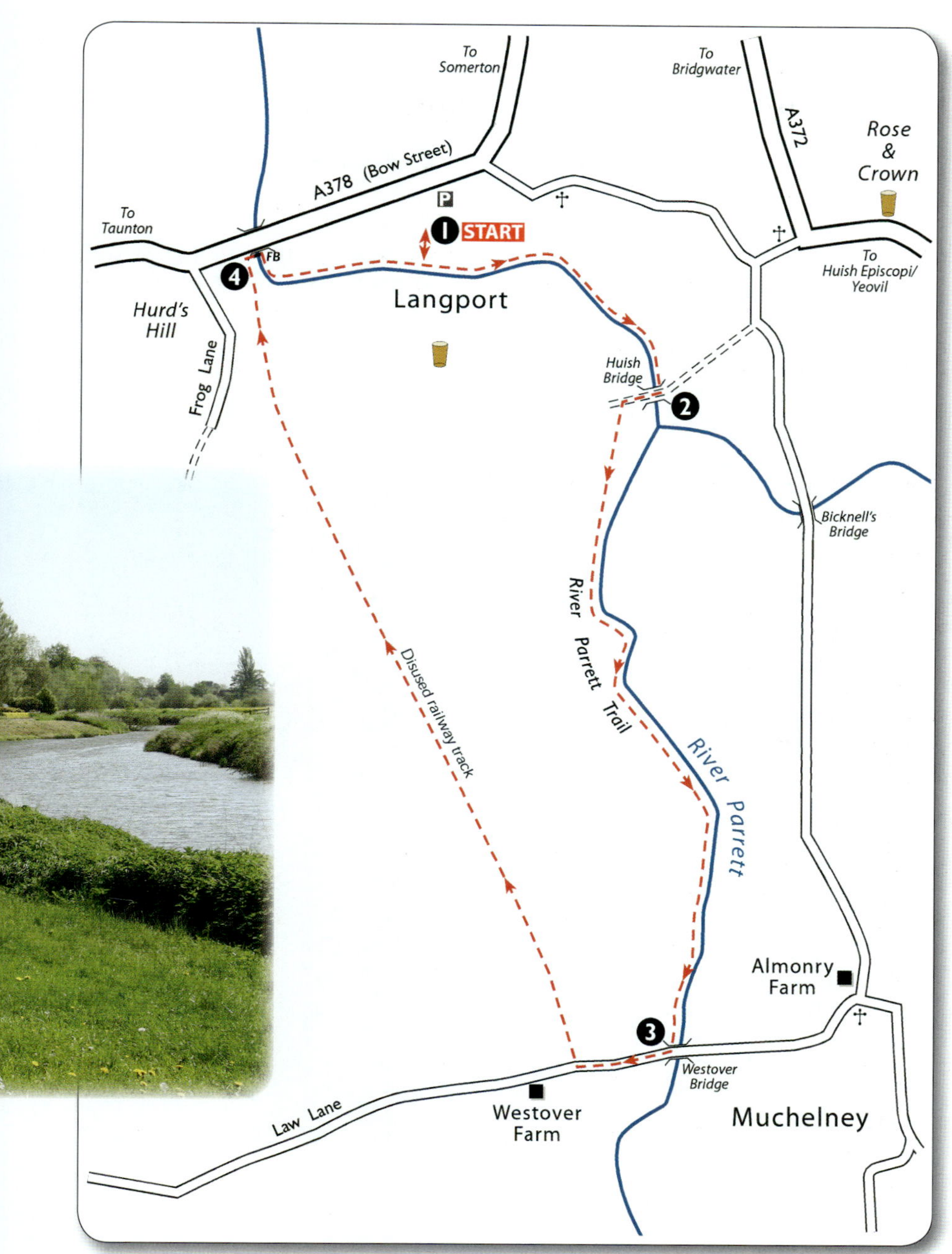
To Somerton
To Bridgwater
A372
Rose & Crown
A378 (Bow Street)
P
START
To Taunton
FB
Langport
4
Hurd's Hill
Frog Lane
Huish Bridge
2
To Huish Episcopi/ Yeovil
Bicknell's Bridge
Disused railway track
River Parrett Trail
River Parrett
Almonry Farm
3
Westover Bridge
Law Lane
Westover Farm
Muchelney

Hamdon Hill Country Park

Carved from the stones of the adjacent quarry, these monoliths provide a useful landmark.

Dominated by deciduous woodland, this is an excelle... for dog owners and is blessed with the dog-welcoming Prince of Wales, a true country inn, at the start and finish. It is ideal for one of those hot summer days where the cool of the trees will be appreciated. For lovers of historic houses, the route can easily be extended to include a visit to Montacute House and Garden where dogs on leads are welcome in the grounds though not in the house itself.

Terrain

Mostly woodland walking, which can be sticky after heavy rain. One short but steep ascent to the top of St Michael's Hill – but a longer but more gradual track can be found to avoid this if required.

Where to park

Free parking at the Hamdon Hill Country Park (GR 478168). Parking close to the inn is for patrons only and is emphasised as 'when using the premises'. Alternative parking can be found on the other side of the road if none is found in the vicinity of the inn. **OS map:** Explorer 129 Yeovil & Sherborne.

How to get there

From the A303 west of Yeovil, turn off on the A356, signposted to Crewkerne. Take the first left, signposted to Stoke Sub Hamdon and drive into the village centre. Turn right, signposted to Ham Hill, and then left, signposted to the Prince of Wales and car parks.

Nearest refreshments

Once serving the needs of the local quarrymen, the 17th-century Prince of Wales sits in its isolated location in the heart of a country park, close to the ranger's office. The top part of the restaurant was formerly the quarrymen's chapel. Dogs are welcome and there is considerable outdoor seating available. The food is ideal for walkers and there is a good selection of real ales. ☎ 01935 822848.

Dog factors

Distance: 2½ miles.
Road walking: None.
Livestock: Possibility of cattle on the short stretches of pasture between points 3 and 4.
Stiles: 2 stiles.
Nearest vets: Kingfisher Veterinary Practice, Martock.

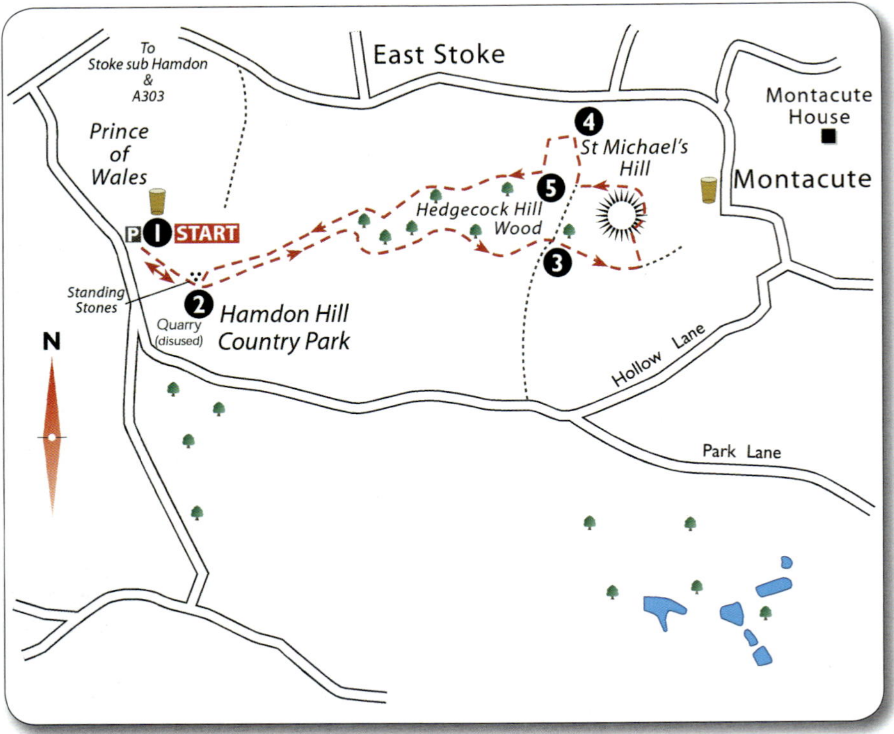

The Walk

1 From the front of the inn, take the signposted path downhill towards **Montacute**. Ignore the footpath to the left, signposted to **East Stoke**, and go ahead with the quarry on your right-hand side. Continue straight ahead as a larger track merges from your right.

2 On reaching two stone carvings in a clearing, there are two paths to your left. Ignore the first, which is signposted '**Montacute** 1¼ miles' and take the second to go past a sign declaring 'Danger steep quarry'. (The quarry is basically safe for four-footed creatures but perhaps not for those with two legs.) These two paths actually run parallel, the left one on the lower ground and the right one (your path) on the higher ground. Continue through an area of dips and banks, indicating former quarrying, into a wood.

The light-yellow stone carved from these quarries has been used all over Somerset but especially in the south of the county. Many of the villages in this area have

The Prince of Wales Inn – a dog-friendly local.

chocolate-box cottages built with this local stone, which mellows to a wonderfully attractive fawn colour.

The path follows a stone wall for part of the way as you walk along the obvious track on the right-hand side of the wood, maintaining the same general direction for about ½ mile. A fenced path then merges from your right (enclosing a wood marked as private). Continue straight ahead, following the fence line, as a wooded knoll rises on your left. Follow the track downhill and as the woodland on your right finishes, ignore the stiled entrance into the field but continue ahead, keeping the field on your right-hand side with the woodland on your left. In ¼ mile, the path forks. Turn right to enter the field over a stile.

3 The wooded **St Michael's Hill** will now be in front of you. Follow the line of telegraph poles to go straight ahead, passing just to the right of the hill, along the right-hand field boundary. Shortly after your track rejoins the edge of the woodland, the path splits. Turn left here to climb towards the tower on top of the hill. The path leads to a T-junction onto a gravel path. Turn left here and follow the path to the summit of the hill.

This steep uphill path can be slippery when wet. At the bottom of the path, it is possible to choose a route with less of an incline, which works its way round the hill more gradually. At the summit there is a tower, which can be ascended with care. It was built as a folly in 1760 by Sir Edward Phelps, the occupant of Montacute House. The Normans had previously built a castle on the top of the hill though no traces remain today.

After a visit to the tower, retrace your steps downhill, ignoring the path to your right, which is the path you ascended earlier. Keep to the path you are on to go down the hill with the higher ground on your left-hand side. You will now be descending the hill on the opposite side to which you went up it. The path comes to a field gate with a stile. Cross this and bear right to a field gate clearly visible at the bottom end of the field.

4 At the bottom of the field, pass through the gate and turn immediately left onto a vehicle track. At a couple of metal-gated entrances, the path bears left and up into the woods. Continue for about 80 yards.

5 Bear right where the path forks. In the field on your right you may be lucky enough to see an ostrich and a couple of alpacas or llamas! You are now walking through shady sycamore woodland, along the right-hand edge of **Hedgecock Hill**. Just after a derelict pumping house, the path splits into twos and threes only to remerge. Ignore a deep gullied uphill path to your left. Shortly after this, ascend the wooden steps with a handrail and turn right onto the path at the top of the steps. Bear left where the path forks at a sign which points back the way you came from **Montacute**. Your route emerges at a crossing of paths with the standing stones before you, which were the ones at point 2 on your outward journey. Turn right here to retrace your steps to the car park.

Ivy Thorn Hill

Along the way.

This short circuit takes in a mix of woodland and field walking and is very pleasant in dry weather. With Ivy Thorn Hill standing proud over the Somerset Levels, the route provides far-reaching views across the dairy lands of central Somerset. It begins with a good woodland run to take the steam out of your dogs before a short stretch of meadowland where leads may be necessary if there are cattle present (usually arable) and finishes with another stretch where well-behaved dogs can run freely off the lead.

Dog factors

Distance: 2 miles.
Road walking: 600 yards of very quiet single track road.
Livestock: Generally none but possible between points 2 and 3.
Stiles: One – but there is a gate alternative alongside.
Nearest vets: Orchard Veterinary Group, Glastonbury.

The view to Dundon Hill from Ivy Thorn Hill.

Terrain

The initial section of about 400 yards includes a steep woodland descent that, although partially provided with steps, can be slippery after wet weather. There is one modest ascent on the return leg. Some field walking is involved but this is very level and good underfoot.

Where to park

The free parking area to the front of Street Youth Hostel on Ivy Thorn Hill (GR 480345). **OS map:** Explorer 141 Cheddar Gorge & Mendip Hills West.

How to get there

From the B3151 just south of Street, at the crest of the hill, take the road west, signposted to Ashcott; the youth hostel will be found on your right-hand side. From the Bridgwater direction, turn right at the Piper's Inn, signposted to Somerton. The youth hostel will be on your left. The official parking area has a narrow entrance but there is alternative parking on the other side of the road in a deep layby.

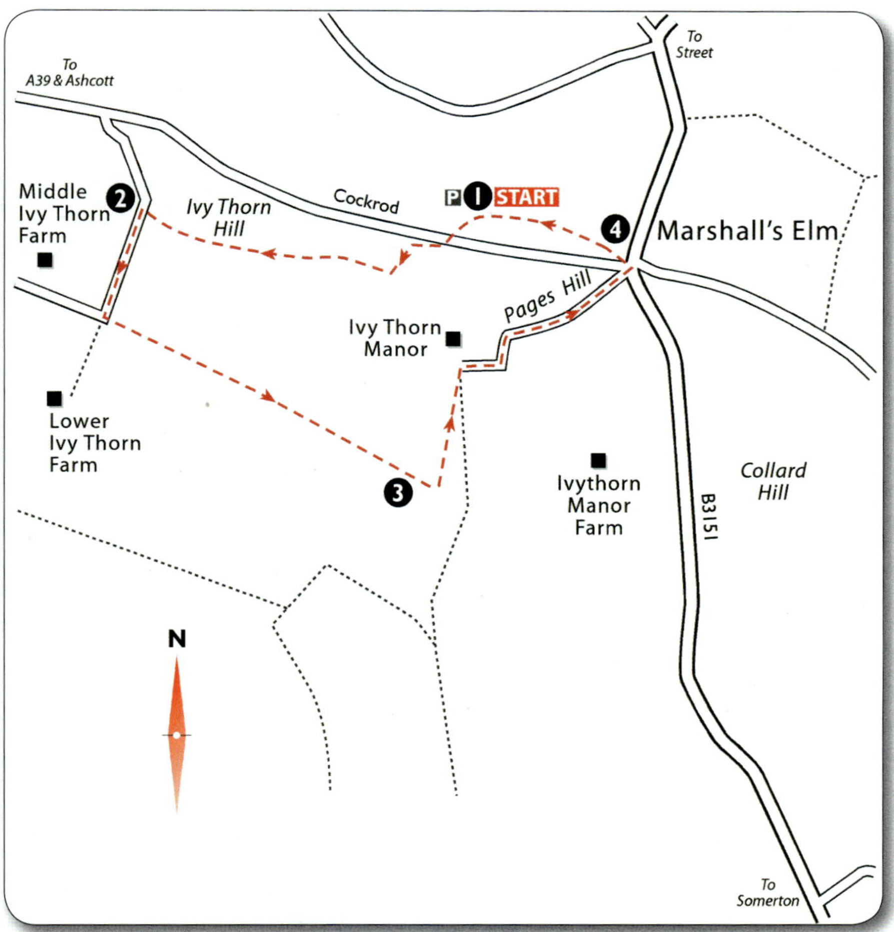

Nearest refreshments

The Castlebrook Inn at Compton Dundon, about a mile south-east of your parking place, is a traditional village pub with a cosy atmosphere. Children and dogs are welcome. It has an inglenook fireplace and was once an old coaching inn dating back to 1540. The restaurant dates back to the 12th century when it served as a medieval hall. Good home-cooked food is served all day and includes a Sunday carvery. The beer garden extends to over an acre. Open from midday to 11 pm except on Mondays (although they describe it as 'open until we shut!'). ☎ 01458 443632.

The Walk

1 From the car park, cross the road into the smaller parking area and turn right into the wood to follow a path parallel to the road through the woodland. In 60 yards take a lesser path, which drops downhill to the left, over wooden steps, bringing you to the woodland edge. Turn right, following the edge, to reach a crossroads of paths at the corner of a field adjacent to the wood. Turn left and immediately right to again follow the woodland edge until you reach a metalled lane.

2 Pass through the kissing gate and turn left onto the lane. In 300 yards, with the track to **Ivy Thorn Farm** in front of you, turn left onto a signposted footpath, following the left-hand field boundary. In ½ mile, after a gate and stile, you reach the corner of an unmetalled road.

3 Continue straight ahead and just before the next gate, turn left onto a green track, heading towards a tall poplar tree. (The OS maps show an official footpath just slightly further on but this is normally barred with electric fencing.) The green track becomes a very quiet minor metalled road as you ascend the hill up to a crossroads at the top of **Pages Hill**.

4 The road to your left is signposted to the youth hostel. Go across this road to the blue-topped waymarkers and turn left, following the blue markers all the way back to the car park.

Shipdam & Dolebury Warren

Rowberrow Bottom.

This is a wonderful walk for dogs and owners alike. Most of the outward leg is through forest where well-behaved dogs can run free, and then comes the open downland of Dolebury Warren with its stunning views to the Bristol Channel. The limited number of stiles are all manageable for small to medium, and large agile, dogs.

Dog factors

Distance: 5¼ miles.
Road walking: 600 yards of very quiet road. The busy A38 also has to be crossed twice.
Livestock: Sheep on second half of Dolebury Warren.
Stiles: All stiles except one have dog-boards, which can be lifted, or gates alongside to offer an alternative. The one exception is just after the start of point 9 and this can be avoided – details later.
Nearest vets: Axe Valley Veterinary Surgery, Cheddar.

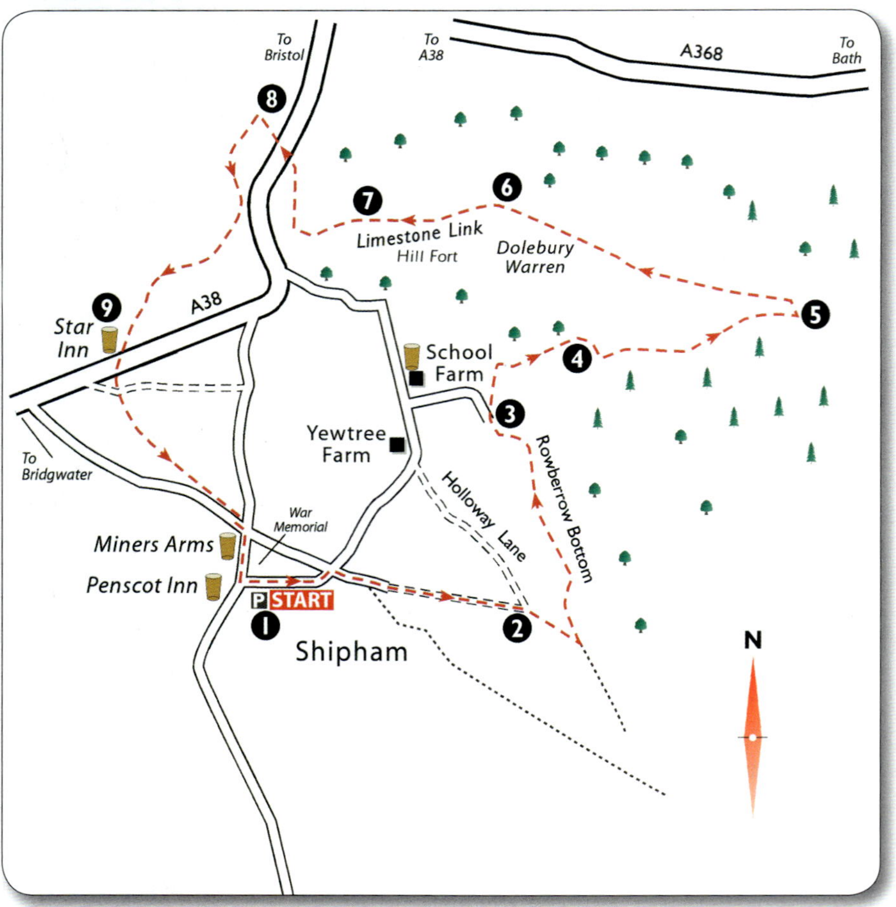

Terrain

Generally firm underfoot even after rain. Moderate inclines only.

Where to park

Roadside parking along Hollow Road in the centre of Shipham village (GR 444575). **OS map:** Explorer 141 Cheddar Gorge & Mendip Hills West.

How to get there

From the A38, to the north of its junction with the A371, turn south-east in the village of Star, signposted to Shipham. In ½ mile, turn right at the crossroads with a school on your right and then in the centre of the village, opposite the Miners Arms, you will see a war memorial to your left. Turn left at the memorial into Hollow Road and take the first available convenient roadside parking space. The lane gets narrower the further along you go.

Nearest refreshments

The Penscot Inn at Shipham. The last time I was there it was proving very popular with groups of walkers who could take advantage of the garden tables on the lawn across the front of the inn, set conveniently away from the village road. Dogs are welcome inside as well as out on the lawn. Food is available daily from 12 noon to 8 pm with the emphasis on fresh, local produce. The Penscot Inn will be found beyond the Miners Arms, on the same side of the road, just before the parish church. ☎ 01934 842659.

The Walk

. . . .

1 Head uphill along **Hollow Road**. At the top of the road, bear right into **Barn Pool**. At the T-junction, turn right into **Lippiatt Lane**, a no through road. Continue ahead, going uphill, as **Lippiatt Lane** becomes a hedge-lined track, to reach a crossroad of tracks where **Holloway Lane** crosses your path.

2 Turn right and immediately left onto the signposted footpath at the '**Rowberrow Warren**' nameboard, signposted as '**Cheddar** 5½', as you continue along the **West Mendip Way**, dropping downhill on a sunken track to reach a stream. Turn left before the stream onto a path signposted to **Rowberrow**. Continue with the stream on your right-hand side until the track becomes a tarred pathway. After two houses and an old limekiln, you reach a third cottage just after which is a gate and a nameboard for **Rowberrow Warren**.

3 Turn right at the cottage, through the gate, to enter the woodland. Go uphill along the track as it bears right to reach the corner of a field area. Bear left here onto a lesser track to gently drop downhill with the field to your right and woodland to your left. Continue ahead, ignoring a track off to the right after the field ends. Then ignore another which doubles back to your left.

1 In 20 yards, turn left to head uphill onto a signposted bridleway. Follow this bold track until another track almost merges in from your left but then actually just runs parallel to your track. Cross over onto that track, keeping the same line of direction to reach a T-junction.

5 Turn left and in 100 yards you reach a gate on the left with a National Trust sign and beyond it the open down of **Dolebury Warren**. Go through the gate (there is a stile alongside) to follow the grassy track along the ridge ahead of you, initially passing along the left-hand side of a fenced enclosure.

6 After the enclosure and after passing through a gate, bear right onto a path signposted with a yellow waymarker as the **Limestone Link**, passing to the right of a stand of tall pine trees. Turn left into the trees at another signposted **Limestone Link** yellow waymarker. Continue through the trees to head along the ridge, aiming for its highest point at the site of the once-huge **Dolebury hill fort**. It would be a sin not to stop here awhile and soak up the views across to the Bristol Channel and beyond.

7 Continue along the same line of direction, passing through the hill fort site and then dropping downhill along a grass track towards woodland. As you enter the wood, you will be faced with three tracks. Take the bolder one to the left, which almost immediately swings to the right to drop down through the woodland. Pass through a gate to leave the woodland and continue downhill on a partly metalled track, passing between cottages to reach the A38 (dogs on lead please, before reaching this busy road).

8 Cross the road to enter a signposted bridleway, heading uphill and to the right to reach a lane in about 150 yards. Turn left onto the lane and follow this track, ignoring all turnings to left and right, to again reach the A38* (dogs on leads, please) at **Star**.

Here you will find the Star Inn, which unfortunately does not cater for dogs.

Dolebury Warren – an ancient hill fort.

9 Cross the road to enter a grass paddock, following the footpath sign as it directs you along the left-hand field boundary to reach the top left corner of the paddock. Cross a stile in the corner* and turn immediately right to reach and cross another stile onto a track. Turn left onto the track and follow it all the way to its end at a metalled road. Turn left at the road and then immediately right at the crossroads to head back to the village centre and the war memorial.

The stile on the last leg is OK for small to medium or large agile dogs. Large cumbersome dogs can avoid this one by turning right when you reach the A38 (see point 8) and then in a short distance turning left onto a stony lane which is the one to follow up to Shipham as described above in point 9.

Bourton Combe

The woodland path in Bourton Combe.

A delightful route through glorious deciduous woodland. Picture those searing-hot days of summer, when no air moves and we seek the respite of shade and the coolness of dense trees. This is the walk for such conditions. It starts by passing Turkey oaks, more normally found in Southern Europe. These can be recognised by the lobes on the leaves being slightly more pointed than the English oak and their acorns have a woolly cup. Entering the woodland of Bourton Combe, you will pass through once-coppiced hazel where the endangered and protected dormouse lives but, being nocturnal and extremely shy, is rarely seen. Watch out for the signs of badgers, which are abundant, roe deer, plenty of squirrels and all the species of woodpeckers.

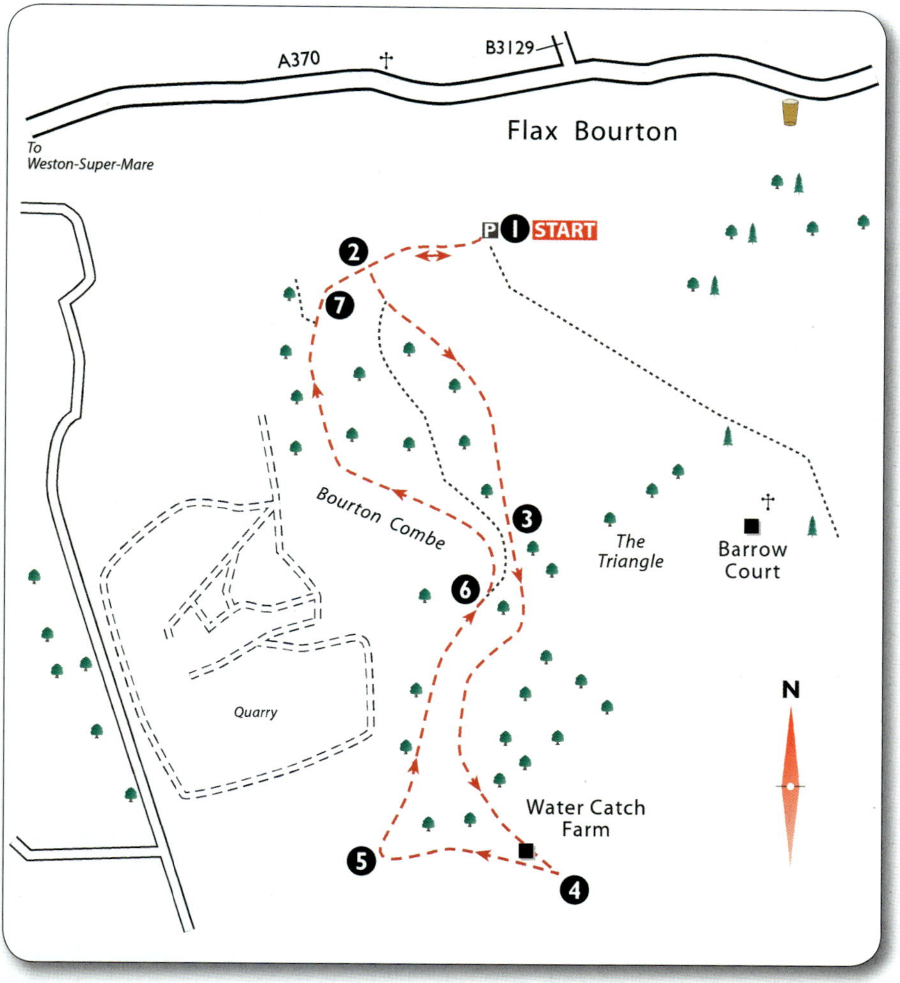

Dog factors

Distance: 2½ miles.
Road walking: None.
Livestock: None.
Stiles: None.
Nearest vets: Dr Susan Yeo, Backwell.

Terrain

Rocky and stony with gentle ascents. Being a woodland walk, it can be damp underfoot in short stretches but there are bypasses aplenty to avoid them.

Where to park

At the far end of Bourton Lane just off the centre of Flax Bourton village (GR 508689). **OS map:** Explorer 154 Bristol West & Portishead.

How to get there

Find the village of Flax Bourton on the A370 between Weston-super-Mare and Bristol. In the centre of the village, to the east of the village church, turn south into Bourton Lane. Park at the far end of the lane.

Nearest refreshments

The Jubilee Inn will be found in the centre of Flax Bourton on the main road to the east of Bourton Lane. Dogs on a lead are allowed in the garden/patio area. ☎ 01275 462797.

An alternative is the recently opened tea rooms at Gatcombe Farm to the east of Flax Bourton. From the village centre, take the B3129 onto Station Road and in ½ mile turn right onto the B3130, Clevedon Road. At the roundabout, take the first exit onto Weston Road and find the farm in ¼ mile.

The view towards Flax Bourton.

This is recommended for those with children since families can sit on the verandah area overlooking the pond and island with its wildfowl including six rheas (emu-like birds from South America) and there is plenty of space for youngsters to run around. For obvious reasons, dogs must be kept on leads. Many of the regular customers here take their dogs with them and tie them up whilst visiting the farm shop and this is quite acceptable to the dog-friendly owners. ☎ 01275 394404.

The Walk

1 From the end of **Bourton Lane**, take the footpath to the right, signposted to **Barrow Common** along an enclosed bower.

2 On reaching a stone wall to your left, turn immediately left to walk along the left-hand side of the wood with fields to your left and following a stone wall on your left. Follow this for just over ¼ mile to a point where the wall turns off to the left to form an area of wood called '**The Triangle**'.

3 Continue straight ahead here and in a short distance go past the corner of a field on your left. Continue ahead as the track curves first right and then left for ¼ mile, eventually reaching **Water Catch Farm** after passing through a gate.

4 You will see a cottage in front of you and then the wall of a farm building. Keep to the left of the building and at the end of it, as you face gates before you, turn sharp right around the building to go past the cottage you saw earlier and with the field on your left. Walk past the entrance to the cottage to go back into the woods along a narrow track, with fields still on your left.

5 As you approach the end of the woodland, you will reach a ruined building on your left and on your right will be a 'Tarmac' sign advising horse riders to dismount when the siren sounds, since they are about to blast in the nearby quarry! Turn right at the sign to go back into the combe and follow the obvious path, with the fields just visible through the trees to your left. Follow the path along the bed of the combe.

6 In just over another ¼ mile, take the left fork, heading downhill to follow a path that runs along the bottom edge of a scree slope after which it curves to the right.

7 On reaching a fork in the track, take the uphill one to the right, and further on at the next fork, turn right and uphill to retrace your steps back to your car.

Charterhouse & Velvet Bottom

Velvet Bottom.

This circuit, high on the Mendips, explores the areas where evidence on the ground tells of the former presence of extensive lead mining activity, dating back to the days of the Romans. Indeed it was almost certainly at Charterhouse that the Romans would have had their local headquarters. Locally, this heavily potted and bumpy landscape is known as 'gruffy' ground which has a very doggy sound to it and is indeed great for dogs to explore, especially towards the end of the walk, where there are rabbit warrens probably as big as any you have ever seen.

The walk passes right through no fewer than three nature reserves, the charmingly named Long Wood, the top end of Black Rock and Velvet Bottom. The first of these is ancient deciduous woodland with pot-holes and caves scattered throughout. A small diversion halfway through this wood reveals the cave known as Rhino Rift where the tooth of a woolly rhinoceros was once discovered. The last reserve through which you pass is almost devoid of trees but offers opportunities to spot lizards, adders, grass snakes and slow worms which sun-bathe on the stony outcrops.

Adders, whilst potentially venomous, are normally only likely to bite if physically disturbed, and then the effect is like that of a serious bee-sting. I have never known a dog to be bitten by a snake on the Mendip Hills but should it happen, then the usual vet's treatment for a severe reaction would involve anti-histamine and antibiotics. My personal experience is that dogs take no interest in adders. I suspect that being cold-blooded, they fail to generate a smell of sufficient interest. Hence, I let my dog run freely – but the choice is yours.

Terrain

The greater part of this walk is along woodland tracks, full of interesting smells for dogs to follow, and through the once heavily-mined grassy moorland with extensive rabbit warrens. The remainder is along tracks or quiet single-track lanes. There are a few gentle inclines. Although there are 6 stiles on this walk, my border collie has always been able to find a 'dog gap' either where one has been built-in or simply 'under the wire'. He has never needed to jump or be lifted over any of the stiles on this walk. Larger, less agile dogs (great danes, wolfhounds) would definitely struggle. For such dogs, the second half of the walk, between point 5 and the end, is absolutely delightful and could be done as an out-and-back walk.

Dog factors

Distance: 4½ miles.
Road walking: 200 yards of very quiet road.
Livestock: Occasionally there are sheep or cattle between points 4 and 5. Sheep are sometimes present in Velvet Bottom for 'conservation grazing'.
Stiles: 6 – see comments above for accessibility.
Nearest vets: Axe Valley Veterinary Practice, Cheddar.

'Gruffy ground' near the parking area.

Where to park

The free public parking area at the Blackmoor lead workings (GR 504556).
OS map: Explorer 141 Cheddar Gorge & Mendip Hills West.

How to get there

On the B3134 to the east of Burrington Combe, take the road signposted south to the village of Charterhouse. Watch out for a modern windmill on your left as you approach a crossroads. Turn left at the crossroads, immediately before the Charterhouse Centre, along a single-track road, to enter the free public parking area at the old Blackmoor lead workings.

Nearest refreshments

The Charterhouse area is almost devoid of civilisation and completely devoid of refreshments! However, there is the very pleasant Riverside Inn, at The Cliffs in nearby Cheddar (5 miles). Dogs are allowed in all areas except the restaurant but meals can be taken in the bars or outside on the patio and in the landscaped garden areas, which slope attractively down to the river. ☎ 01934 742452.

Another pleasant spot, just across the river from the Riverside Inn, is the Edelweiss Restaurant and Tea Rooms which has outside seating alongside the river and dog water bowls are provided. This will be found on the left-hand side as you enter Cheddar on the Gorge road and there is parking for customers. ☎ 01934 742347.

The Walk

. . . .

1 From the car park, turn left to follow a track heading north, passing through a gate in front of you and with the distant wireless station masts diagonally to your left. Follow the path as it curves to the left until reaching a signposted winding track, which crosses your path. Turn left onto that track, crossing a small dam, footbridge and stile to reach the metalled road.

2 Turn right onto the road and in 70 yards take the turning to the left at a '**Townsend**' sign and indicated as a public bridleway. Carry on up this quiet road to reach the radio transmitter masts.

3 Take the significant track to the left of the wireless station masts. Continue along this straight green lane, going downhill to a point where a footpath that crosses your track is marked with yellow arrows on the stiles either side of the lane.

4 Turn left, crossing the wooden stile, and head forward and downhill to reach an excavated gully into which runs spring water from a pipe. This is the source of a stream that you will follow all the way down to the road, keeping it on your right-hand side. In just over ½ mile, cross a stile (do not cross the stile immediately to your right) and from here follow the right-hand field boundaries, finally heading towards the right-hand of two buildings to reach the road.

5 Turn right at the road and in 50 yards go to the left at an obvious fork onto a no through road. In just a few yards, turn left onto a track and then at the bottom of a dip pass through a gate to enter a field. Turn right and follow a track which heads near the right-hand field boundary to reach and cross another stile. Continue on the route leading down into the **Long Wood Nature Reserve**, following the obvious path, which curves to the left, for ¾ mile. At the end of the wood, continue past an interpretation panel, to a junction of paths just before a National Trust sign for '**Black Rock Gorge**'.

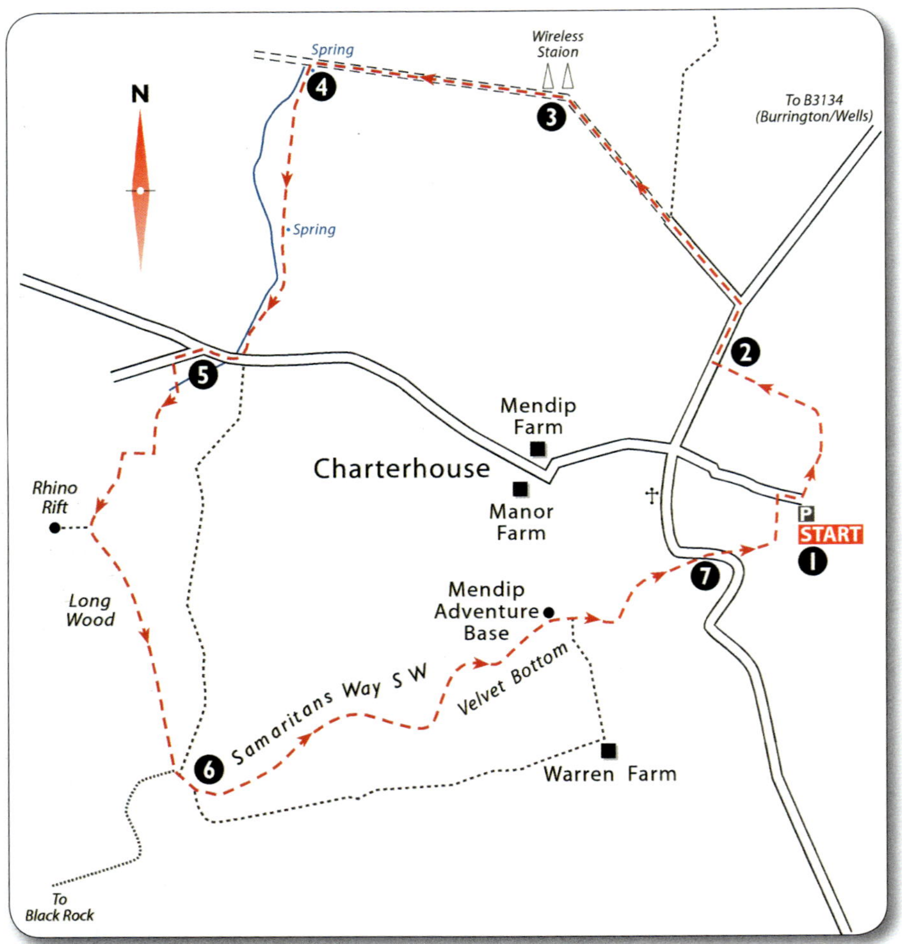

6 Turn left through a kissing gate to enter the **Velvet Bottom Nature Reserve**, which is marked with its own interpretation panel. In a few yards, cross the remains of a stone wall to follow the obvious path through **Velvet Bottom**. You will pass through a landscape of stony outcrops, rabbit warrens and deep depressions where lead mines once existed. You will reach the **Mendip Adventure Base hut** where a path goes off to the left. Continue straight ahead to reach the metalled road.

7 At the road, go straight across to follow the waymarked footpath over the rough ground and in less than ¼ mile you will reach the car park.

Baltonsborough

A riverside hay meadow at Baltonsborough.

A **very pleasant**, absolutely level walk over easy terrain, taking advantage of stream and riverside paths through meadows. Although there are 16 stiles to be negotiated on the route, they all proved very easy for my border collie and would do so for any small or medium size dog.

Baltonsborough is famed locally as the birthplace of St Dunstan, a former Abbot of Glastonbury who was to become the Archbishop of Canterbury. He was one of those early abbots to whom we owe our gratitude for the drainage of so much of the low-lying land in Somerset and it was here at Baltonsborough that he began that work. He ensured that the River Brue was capable of draining the moors and was responsible for introducing the Mill Stream, the course of which this walk follows.

Dog factors

Distance: 4 miles.
Road walking: ¾ mile on a quiet country lane.
Livestock: Possibility of dairy cattle albeit normally only in a couple of fields out of the many through which the walk passes.
Stiles: There are 16 stiles but all are passable for dogs up to medium size, otherwise 3½ ft high to jump over. My border collie easily slips under all the stiles or the gates alongside.
Nearest vets: Orchard Veterinary Group, Glastonbury.

Terrain

Very level walking along grassy tracks through pasture land, alongside river and stream. Firm underfoot in all seasons. Some road walking but only on very quiet lanes.

Where to park

Roadside parking in Church Walk, Baltonsborough (GR 542348). **OS map:** Explorer 141 Cheddar Gorge & Mendip Hills West.

Buster on the bridge over the mill stream.

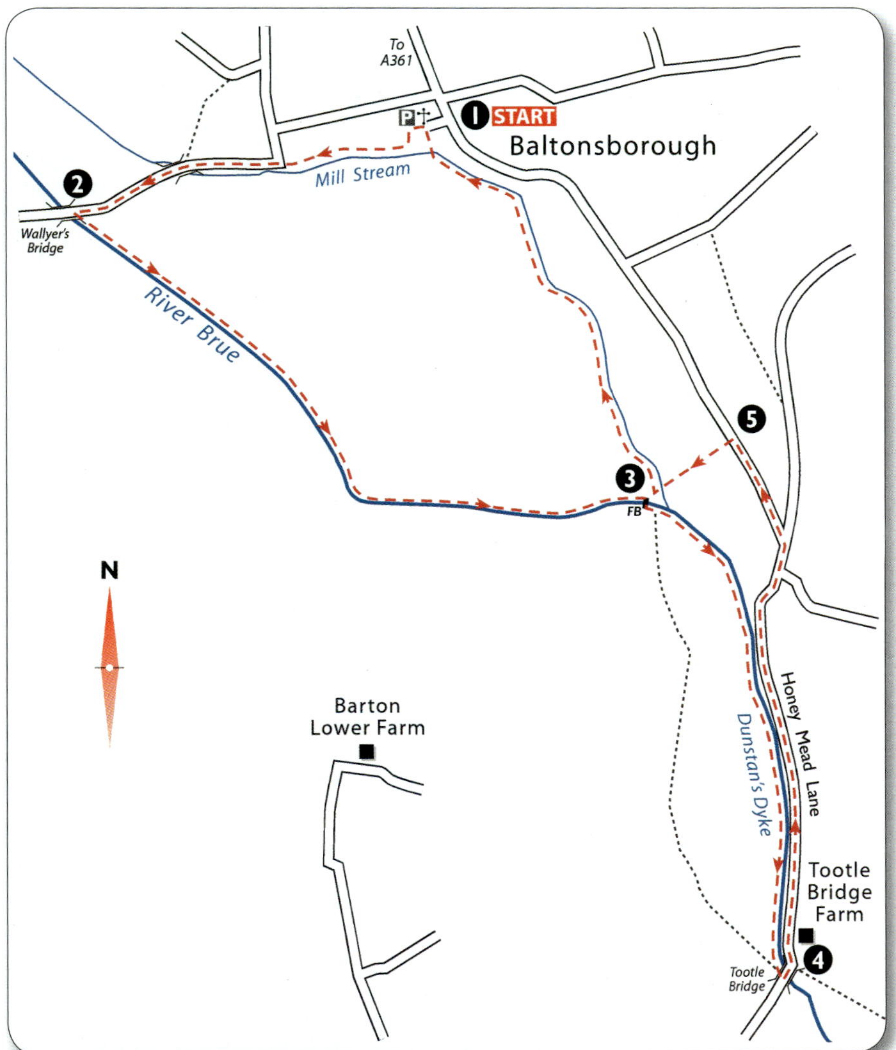

How to get there

From West Pennard, which is on the A361 to the east of Glastonbury, take the minor road south, signposted to Baltonsborough. Follow the signs to a crossroads in the village with the Greyhound Inn on your right-hand side. Go straight across and turn almost immediately right in to Church Walk, a no-throughroad leading to the village church.

Nearest refreshments

The village pub is the Greyhound Inn, which is to be found at the crossroads in the centre of the village. Dogs on leads are welcome inside. but no meals are served. Open every evening from 6.30 pm but only at lunchtimes on weekends (no meals). ☎ 01458 850485.

For those seeking a meal, the Lion at Pennard will be found back at the A361 in West Pennard. This is a 17th-century coaching house, complete with flagstone floors, inglenook fireplaces with wintertime log fires and old beams to complete the traditional inn image. For dog walkers there is ample seating in the gardens and water bowls are available. It's a warm, friendly, welcoming place and an ideal stopping place for walkers. ☎ 01458 832941.

The Walk

. . . .

1 Go through the churchyard, passing to the left of the church. At the rear of the church, leave the churchyard through the stone archway with its kissing gate and enter a field. Turn left in the field to reach the **Mill Stream** and then turn right to walk with the stream on your left-hand side to reach the road after passing through one more kissing gate. Turn left onto the road and in ¼ mile, after crossing the **Mill Stream**, you reach **Wallyer's Bridge** where it crosses the **River Brue**.

2 Turn left over a stile just before the bridge, onto the signposted footpath. Follow the bank of the **River Brue** for almost a mile to reach the second of two weirs where the **Brue** meets the **Mill Stream**.

3 Turn right through a kissing gate to use the footbridge to cross over the **River Brue**. Then, after passing through a second kissing gate, turn left to walk along the raised bank of **Dunstan's Dyke** with the **Brue** now on your left-hand side all the way down to **Tootle Bridge**.

4 Cross the bridge and turn left onto the very quiet road, which leads back towards **Baltonsborough**. In about ½ mile, ignore the two turnings off to the right. About 300 yards after the second right turn, cross a stile on the left to take the track indicated as a public footpath, which leads to the **Mill Stream**. Go straight ahead across the meadow to reach a footbridge, which can clearly be seen just to the right of a large willow.

5 Cross the **Mill Stream** using the footbridge and dog-friendly stiles. Turn right to follow the **Mill Stream** back to the church where you turn right over one last bridge to pass through the churchyard and return to your car.

Castle Cary

The Round House once served as the lock-up.

This short walk falls into three distinct phases, the uphill outward leg with increasingly extensive views, the fairly level middle section providing a fine panorama over Castle Cary and across to the Mendip Hills, and the homeward downhill leg passing through the site of the medieval castle from which the town takes its name. As you descend the hill, to the left of the castle site, is Park Pond, a small lake which the locals know as the Horse Pond and which is the source of the River Cary and once the town's water supply. The walk takes advantage of Lodge Hill, which overlooks the town, providing views to North Somerset, Dorset and Wiltshire.

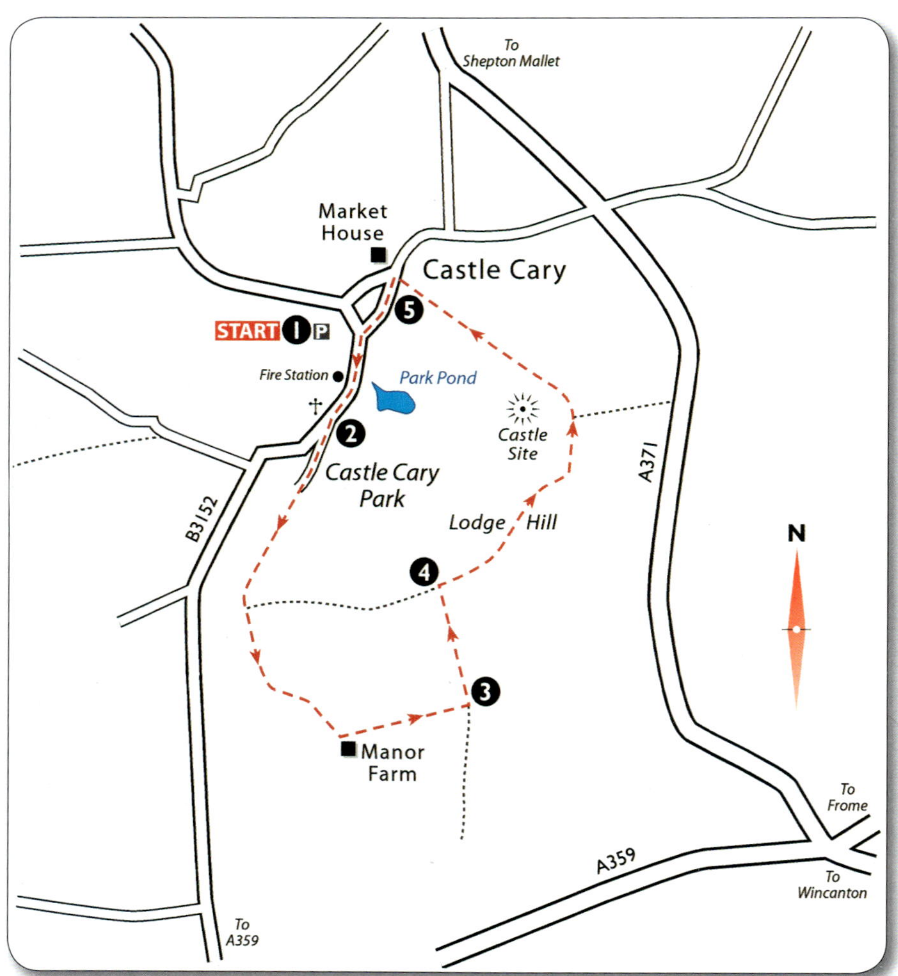

Dog factors

Distance: 2 miles.
Road walking: 500 yards of town road, with pavement all the way.
Livestock: Cattle possible between points 4 and 5.
Stiles: None – kissing gates only.
Nearest vets: Delaware Veterinary Group, Castle Cary.

Castle Cary from Lodge Hill.

Terrain

The outward leg gently climbs uphill along a gravel track before entering the grassland of the fields along Lodge Hill. The return leg is more steeply down a grassy slope, and when damp underfoot it may be preferable to finish the walk by retracing your steps from the bench seats between points 4 and 5.

Where to park

At the Mildbrook Gardens free public car park, off Park Street (GR 639322). **OS map:** Explorer 142 Shepton Mallet &Mendip Hills East.

How to get there

Castle Cary is 5 miles north-west of Wincanton, just off the A371, on the road to Shepton Mallet. Entering the village from the south on the B3152, the Mildbrook Gardens free public car park will be found on the left-hand side next to the fire station. If approaching from the Shepton Mallet direction, turn right at the T-junction and turn right before the fire station.

Somerset - A Dog Walker's Guide

Nearest refreshments

The Horse Pond Inn, just north of the car park, allows well-behaved dogs inside on leads. It is a freehouse and is open daily from 10.30 am to 11 pm, or midnight on Fridays and Saturdays. Bar snacks and restaurant meals are served. ☎ 01963 359364.

The Walk

1 From the car park, return to the B3152 and turn right onto **Park Street**.

2 Turn left into **The Park** (not Park Place), which is a lane running across the front of the primary school opposite the parish church, and is signposted 'Orientation Point – **Lodge Hill**'. Follow this no through road up the slope until the path becomes a gravel farm track. Ignore the signposted footpath to the left at the back of some houses. Continue along the track as it bears left and passes a group of barns to the right, then a complex of barns to the left and finally a third group as you continue uphill. Views will now have opened up all around you.

3 Turn left after this last group of barns to enter a wide-gated field. Follow the left-hand field boundary to the field corner to pass through a kissing gate into a field, which slopes away in front of you with views to **Glastonbury Tor** and the **Mendip Hills** beyond.

4 Turn right to follow the right-hand field boundary along the obvious path across the top of the slope.

There is a convenient bench here on which to sit and admire the views across Castle Cary. You will also find an observation platform with a free-to-use telescope and an interpretation plaque that shows the directions of all the surrounding hills and landmarks.

Pass through a kissing gate (marked with a yellow disc) into the next field. Continue straight ahead past two more benches until you start your descent back to **Castle Cary**, eventually reaching the site of the castle.

5 In the bottom corner of the final field, pass through a kissing gate to follow steps downhill onto a tarmac path leading into the town centre where you will be facing the **Market House** across the road (around the back of the Market House will be found the **Round House**, the old town lock-up). Turn left here to retrace your steps to the car park.

Bathford Hill

Squirrel watching on Bathford Hill.

Partly in the old county of Somerset and partly in Wiltshire, this walk is just 5 miles from the centre of Bath, and yet is deep into the countryside with stunning views as you stroll through ancient woodlands. The circuit starts out along the top edge of a steep-sided wooded valley, following the county boundary. Along the bottom of the valley runs the meandering River Avon as it cuts its wide loops through the landscape. One short stretch of main road walking, just 200 yards, conveniently comes after over a mile of woodland by which time your dogs should have run off that initial burst of energy. A return leg passes through fields before re-entering the Bathford Hill woodlands where again your dogs can run free before returning to the car park.

Dog factors

Distance: 4¼ miles.
Road walking: 140 yards of main road (with verge), 600 yards of quiet unclassified road.
Livestock: None generally over what is arable farmland. Horses in the paddock just after point 5 on the walk. These have always minded their own business and completely ignored my dog. However, out of courtesy at least, please keep your dogs on a lead over this section.
Stiles: Four but all manageable.
Nearest vets: Harris Hill and Gibbons, Bradford-on-Avon.

Terrain

Mostly level with gentle slopes. Stony and clay-earth tracks through woodland with clay-earth footpaths over fields.

Looking over the Avon valley.

Where to park

The free car park on the minor road between Bathford and Monkton Farleigh (GR 797663). **OS maps:** Explorer 155 Bristol & Bath and 156 Chippenham & Bradford-on-Avon (the walk crosses over the boundaries of these two maps).

How to get there

To the east of Bath, take the A363 between Batheaston and Bradford-on-Avon. Turn onto the minor road north-east, signposted to Monkton Farleigh. In the village centre, turn left, signposted to Farleigh Rise. In ½ mile continue straight ahead where Farleigh Rise goes off to your right, past a '6 foot 6 inches' width limit sign. In a short distance you will find the free public car park on your left.

Nearest refreshments

The Muddy Duck at Monkton Farleigh, which is passed on the route, is charmingly set and well worth a visit. They welcome dogs on leads in the bar area, plus there is ample outside seating in the attractive courtyard and splendid gardens. Inside you will find a log fire to warm those winter days. Opinions differ as to the age of this hostelry but its presence here for several centuries at least is beyond dispute and provides evidence of its consistency over the years. ☎ 01225 858705; website: www.kingsarms-bath.co.uk.

The Walk

● ●

1 Leave the car park, going past the **Brown's Folly** interpretation panel. In just a few yards, at a T-junction of paths, turn right (the path to your left is your return route). Follow the path, which winds through the woodland, ignoring one that slopes up to your left. The track, with the ground sloping rapidly down on your right-hand side, curves around to the left, leading you to a kissing gate. Pass through the gate to reach a clearing with magnificent views over the Avon valley. At the end of the clearing, pass through another kissing gate into the woodland.

2 Continue straight ahead along the main track through the woodland ignoring all diversions to left and right, until you reach the busy main road (dogs on leads!). Turn left and follow the road for about 140 yards. Walk on the left-hand side of the road where there is a wide-enough verge to keep you away from the traffic.

3 Turn left onto a bridleway alongside the gated entrance to **Dry Arch House**. The bridleway rises up from a track that runs under the main road. In about 80 yards, follow the track as it turns right to reach the metalled road at **Douch Farm Nursery**. Go straight across into a narrow lane, turning right at the **Pinckney Green** sign into a lane.

4 At the end of the lane, pass through a kissing gate and turn left to enter the field via a seven-bar gate with an overgrown stile at its side. Go straight ahead across the field, heading for its top left corner as you pass to the right of field stables. Exit the field via a stile with a dog gate on its right. In the next field, look straight ahead to see a kink in the hedge line. Head just to the right of this to enter the next field. Follow the left-hand field boundary to the end of the field. Cross another stile into a paddock and follow the right-hand boundary to leave the paddock by another stile in just 15 yards. Cross another stile into a short track to reach a cross-track. Keep straight ahead here, aiming for the telegraph pole just to the right of the church tower, to reach a track as it makes a right-angle bend where you join it.

5 Keep straight ahead along the same line of direction, following the track along the back of a housing estate to your left and a field to your right. Just beyond the estate, and as you approach a large barn to your right, look for a gate on your left-hand side. Just past the field gate, turn left through a pedestrian gate to enter a paddock. Bear right to cross the paddock, heading towards the near end of a long, low barn. Turn left just before reaching the barn wall, following a track that runs around the back of the barn alongside the church wall at **Monkton Farleigh**. Stay on that track to reach the quiet village road.

6 Turn left, heading uphill through the centre of the village, ignoring turnings left and right, to head towards **Farleigh Rise** past the **Muddy Duck**.

7 In ¼ mile turn left, using the stile or field gate, into a field. Go straight ahead, following the right-hand field boundary. Keeping to the same line of direction, enter the next field and follow the left-hand field boundary to reach a track that crosses your path. Go straight across, keeping exactly the same line of direction, to pass through a small wood. As you leave the woodland, turn left onto a crossing track and then, almost immediately where the track turns left, you go straight ahead, back onto your former line of direction, heading for a gate which leads into the main woodland straight ahead.

8 Pass through the gate to follow a walled path. At the end of the walled section, turn right to follow the wall with it on your right-hand side. Follow this all the way to **Brown's Folly**, a towering column. Its presence creates a break in the wall but continue straight ahead and the wall will reappear. Continue following the wall, which eventually turns to the right. Shortly after, it disappears again, at the site of a giant hole, but keep straight ahead and it reappears once again for you to follow almost all the way back to the car park. Just as the road becomes visible in front of you, look to the left for the steps down to the car park in just a few yards.

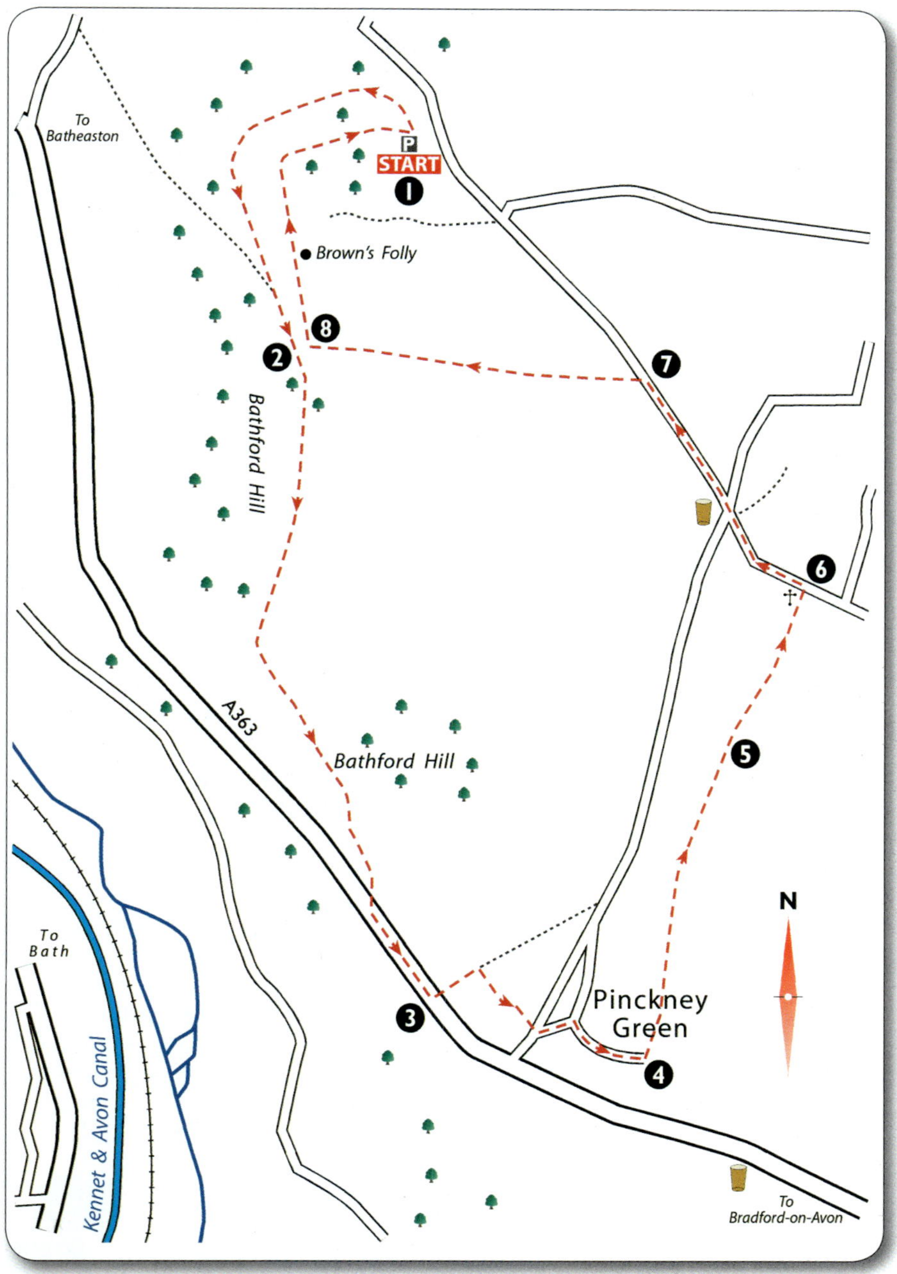
To Batheaston
P
START
1
Brown's Folly
8
2
Bathford Hill
7
6
A363
5
Bathford Hill
3
N
Pinckney Green
4
To Bath
Kennet & Avon Canal
To Bradford-on-Avon

APPENDIX

Small Animal Veterinary Practices

The following are all veterinary practices that are close to the walks described. They have been selected as handling small animals and dogs in particular.

Axe Valley Veterinary Practice

Greystone House, Union Street, Cheddar, Somerset BS27 3NA ☎ 01934 741292

Delaware Veterinary Group

Fulford House, Torbay Road, Castle Cary, Somerset BA7 7DT ☎ 01963 350307

Dulverton Veterinary Practice

The Veterinary Centre, Bridge Street, Dulverton, Somerset TA22 9HJ
☎ 01398 323285

Harris Hill & Gibbons

Prospect House, Frome Road, Bradford-on-Avon, Wiltshire BA15 1LA
☎ 01225 862656

Kingfisher Veterinary Practice

Martock Veterinary Centre, Stapleton Road, Martock, Somerset TA12 6HH
☎ 01935 825199

The Langport Veterinary Clinic

Regency House, Bow Street, Langport, Somerset TA10 9PS ☎ 01458 250459

Orchard Veterinary Group

Wirrall Park Road, Glastonbury, Somerset BA6 9XE ☎ 01458 832972

Quantock Veterinary Hospital

Cheetham House, The Drove, Bridgwater, Somerset TA6 4BA ☎ 01278 450080
Quantock Veterinary Hospital also has a surgery in Castle Street, Nether Stowey, which is served by the same telephone number.

Neil Rudram Ltd

17 Canon Street, Taunton, TA1 1SW ☎ 01823 271042
Neil Rudram deals entirely with small pets, dogs in particular.

Smith & Partners

Manor Gardens Veterinary Centre, Berrow Road, Burnham-on-Sea, Somerset, TA8 2ET ☎ 01278 794794

White Lodge Veterinary Clinic

Stephenson Road, Minehead, Somerset TA24 5EB ☎ 01643 703649

Dr Susan Yeo

44 Rodney Road, Backwell, Bristol BS48 3HW ☎ 01275 462691